The Widow's ~~Mite~~ *Might*

CJP Navarro

 Published by Faithless Daughter Ministries, LLC.
P.O. Box 644, Columbus, NC 28722.

Author photo by Cassy Mirich Photography

Cover photo by Jesse

Cover art by CJPN

The Widow's Might

Written by: CJP Navarro

Faithless Daughter Ministries, LLC.

Dedicated to the most faithful woman I know.
Mom.
Here's to you!

All my love, c.

Acknowledgements:

To my husband, my forever best friend, thank you for everything.

To my mom, thank you for allowing me an attempt at your remarkable story. You bring hope to everyone who meets you. I pray this book will give others a glimpse of the woman I know and love.

And to Nancy, an avid reader and friend who catches everything I don't, gives valuable insight, tells me what I need to hear, and oh yes, who also happens to be my mom-in-law. Thank you for reading!

To Paula, a faithful coworker and friend who is loved more than words could express. I am forever grateful for your thoughts and encouragement over the years and for you now taking the time to care about my little writing project. I love you dearly my friend. You are loved more than you could possibly know by all of us. Looking so forward to a happy reunion with Bob, who I know is currently boasting the brightest smile in Heaven…

Table of Contents:

Introduction:

The Widow's Mite

Have you ever wondered about the woman in the story of the bible known as the Widow's Mite*? In the King James Version, the book of Mark tells a very short, but very remarkable account of a poor widow giving two copper coins called 'mites' to the offering. These two coins barely made a penny by today's standards, and yet this was all the money she had in the world. Often, I would hear sermons on this passage of scripture where the focus would tend to gravitate toward the rich people giving out of their abundance. As the preacher would go on preaching to us 'rich' people about giving more, I found myself drawn to her. Who was this remarkable woman? What was her story?*

As I pondered about this hidden woman of scripture, I suddenly realized I actually knew her! This faithful widow who gave all she had to live on is my own dear mom. The truly remarkable widow deserving praise. I pray you will be as blessed by her story as I am.

Love, c.

Chapter 1:

Meet Joan

Joan in Hebrew means 'heroine' and 'God-loving.' It is comical how someone's name can fit them so well. My mother has always been my hero. That may sound like such a cliché, but it's true.

As a very young child my dad was my hero. But when he died, I watched my thirty-seven-year-old widowed mother come to life in a way that I hope words can explain. Her faithfulness in taking care of us kids is overwhelming to ponder. I can't get over her strong resolve and stubbornness to never give up. No one came to our rescue. No one, but my mom. She was our rock. She kept us going when we were paralyzed with fear. She fought for us when we strayed onto dark paths. She worked long hours with a smile on her face. She helped those in need, though our need was just as great. She was our biggest fan and loudest cheerleader. She was faithful for as long as we needed her.

Her life has been marked with great suffering. Yet, her light shines brighter still. Her smile is famously radiant with clear blue eyes that really do sparkle. Now in her sixties she looks as youthful as ever. Strangers open-up to her and can't get enough. They are drawn to her light like a moth to a flame. Children run to her to be kissed and cuddled. Knowing there is safety in her arms. Disgruntled adults melt in her presence and depart as life-long friends. Her children rise up and call her blessed. She is a walking, breathing, 'Proverbs 31 Woman' in the flesh.

An excellent wife who can find?
She is far more precious than jewels.
The heart of her husband trusts in her,
and he will have no lack of gain.

She does him good, and not harm,
all the days of her life.

She seeks wool and flax,
and works with willing hands.
She is like the ships of the merchant;
she brings her food from afar.

She rises while it is yet night
and provides food for her household
and portions for her maidens.

She considers a field and buys it;
with the fruit of her hands she plants a vineyard.

She dresses herself with strength
and makes her arms strong.

She perceives that her merchandise is profitable.
Her lamp does not go out at night.
She puts her hands to the distaff,
and her hands hold the spindle.

She opens her hand to the poor
and reaches out her hands to the needy.
She is not afraid of snow for her household,
for all her household are clothed in scarlet.
She makes bed coverings for herself;
her clothing is fine linen and purple.

Her husband is known in the gates
when he sits among the elders of the land.
She makes linen garments and sells them;
she delivers sashes to the merchant.

Strength and dignity are her clothing,
and she laughs at the time to come.

She opens her mouth with wisdom,
and the teaching of kindness is on her tongue.
She looks well to the ways of her household
and does not eat the bread of idleness.

Her children rise up and call her blessed;
her husband also, and he praises her;

"Many women have done excellently,
but you surpass them all."

Charm is deceitful, and beauty is vain,
but a woman who fears the LORD is to be praised.
Give her of the fruit of her hands,
and let her works praise her in the gates.
Proverbs 31:10-31

My mom epitomizes the infamous 'Proverbs 31 Woman'. As an adult I now marvel at her and wonder about her story. This skinny, malnourished country girl who grew up to marry a rolling-stone that she barely knew. This painfully shy, incredibly beautiful, and extremely intelligent girl who has become our town jewel. This is the widow Jesus saw in the temple that day. The widow who faithfully, quietly put in her two mites barely worth a penny. Yet, Jesus noticed just how big her sacrifice really was. And He blessed her for it.

But, before the blessing came the storm. Before the woman we see today there was heart-ache beyond belief.

That last night together was sweet. Life had been hard. Mistakes had been made and forgiveness needed to be asked. By both husband and wife. They wanted to make up. They wanted to continue. To persevere and raise their growing family together. To put the pieces back together. That night they said they were sorry. They made up. Like a thousand couples before them. Two souls being molded into one in the midst of a broken world. The last few years had been hard for Joan. How could she know the next few would prove even harder? The hopeful couple that night didn't know it would be their last.

The morning came, and Joan became our young widow to a murdered husband.

Tom stood in his upstairs bathroom taking his last toke as he stared into the woods beyond the house; Joan made pancakes downstairs. She smiled as Tom came downstairs and sat down to eat his breakfast. Her eyes full of joy as she watched him laughing with their only son, who was just over three. Tom's pride and joy. How sweet it was to see the proud, young daddy sharing hot pancakes with his smiling toddler.

He had told Joan how much he wanted a son even before their wedding day. Ironically, that son didn't come until after Tom was first arrested for drug-trafficking. The beginning of the end for him. True joy in having his boy, shadowed by too many mistakes catching up at once. Still, the joy was there for Tom and Joan she reflected that morning. Despite the cloud they couldn't get away from, there was laughter and joy. Young dad and his son laughed together now, sharing pancakes. Tom looking as handsome as ever in the light blue sweater she had found recently at a local thrift store in her frugality.

When Tom finally jumped up to leave he kissed his boy, his 5-month-old daughter, his beautiful trophy wife, nodded a good-bye to his mother-in-law and grabbed his crutches. Their three older daughters already gone to school. Joan knew he was in a rush to get to his 9 o'clock appointment. Tom the salesman. Tom the Real Estate Developer. Tom the builder. Tom the entrepreneur. He was good at what he did. And Joan had been right there with him from the very beginning. In the failing and the succeeding. She had always been his perfect helper. The perfect Proverbs 31 wife.

That morning there was hope filling her heart. Their marriage was stronger than ever. Despite all the difficulties. Despite the mistakes and heart-ache. When Tom looked at her that last time, he knew what he had in her. Her faithfulness was steady and sure. He left their home feeling like the lucky man that he was.

But, his time had come. They were waiting for him at the bottom of that long drive-way. Hiding out in the forever extending forest surrounding their home. Knowing the nearest neighbor was over a mile away.

Knowing no one would be looking. Knowing they wouldn't be caught. Joan later wondered if her husband somehow knew as he stood in that bathroom staring into the trees, feeling the eyes on him, knowing he was out of time.

But, that morning Joan never heard a thing. As she cleaned up breakfast and began loading the laundry to take to town for cleaning at the laundry mat, nothing seemed amiss. Until the phone rang. It was the office secretary wanting to know where Tommy was. It was after 9 o'clock and he had never showed. Mysteriously neither had the new customers who had scheduled the appointment.

'He must have gotten a flat,' thought Joan, which often happened on the miles of dirt road they had to drive to get to the office that was close to town.

Sadly, Joan was wrong about the flat tire. As she drove down the long, winding driveway in the Jeep Waggoneer packed with dirty laundry, her three-year-old son, her 5-month-old daughter, and her mentally-ill mom, Joan's heart stopped as she came to a halt behind

Tommy's old blue pick-up truck. Both doors wide open. Crutches in the back.

Slowly she opened her Jeep door and slid out silently. Silence. Nothing moved. Except Joan as she creeped toward something lying beside the truck.

Suddenly she froze. She knew. She saw the light blue sweater on the lifeless body. Her husband of nineteen years. Her adventurous Tommy. Gone.

All she could think was how final death was. The shock of it hit her hard as she mechanically slid back into her Jeep and expertly backed up the driveway, barely seeing the road through her tears. Her mother didn't say a word. The kids didn't make a whimper. They must have known, too. There was only silence as Joan made the call to the authorities who were not surprised.

Joan shouldn't have been surprised either. Tommy had been telling her this would happen. He had been forced to help the authorities catch the big fish they really wanted. Young Tom was small bait when they caught him and used him to get to that big catch. He never told Joan they had begged him to take his young family and hide in witness protection. But the authorities assured her when she questioned them that they did offer it to him in exchange for his cooperation, but he refused. He didn't think living in constant hiding was living at all.

The days after her husband's death left Joan's head spinning. She couldn't catch her breath, but somehow life had to go on. Her five young children needed her. She couldn't have stopped if she had wanted to. Revenge filled her mind. But life spun her along. Her heart laid bare. How could this happen? She was left with nothing but a pile of debts to be paid, children to feed and clothe, and a struggling business to run.

And here is where our heroine is truly born. The widow's might comes to full fruition. My mom stood firm in the face of adversity. When others would run away in fear. She would stand firm. When others would lose faith. She would be faithful still. And when others would turn a blind eye. She would know God still cared.

And [Jesus] sat down opposite the treasury
and watched the people putting money
into the offering box.

Many rich people put in large sums.
And a poor widow came
and put in two small copper coins,
which make a penny.

And he called his disciples to him
and said to them,

"Truly, I say to you,
this poor widow has put in more
than all those who are contributing
to the offering box.

For they all contributed out of their abundance,
but she out of her poverty
has put in everything she had,
all she had to live on."
Mark 12:41-44

I always wanted to know more about this widow. I wondered at her story. Wondered about her. Marveled at her faithfulness. Then I realized, this widow is my mother. And I know her story well. Come and meet her. Joan. Our God-loving heroine. For she is truly a wonder to behold.

Chapter 2: The Excellent Wife

An excellent wife who can find?
She is far more precious than jewels.

The heart of her husband trusts in her,
and he will have no lack of gain.

She does him good, and not harm,
all the days of her life.
Proverbs 31:10-12

When Tom met Joan he practically screamed at the sight of her. She went whirling past him rocking her 'Daisy Dukes' as she effortlessly skated around that little roller rink hidden away, deep in the hills of north Georgia. Her long, straight blonde hair flowing behind her as she whizzed by. He was mesmerized.

It was May 12, 1972. The day after Joan's eighteenth birthday. Her entire family had forgotten all about it. As she relayed her sad story to this new-comer he promised her that he would never forget a thing like her birthday. His smooth talk and flashy smile were a stark contrast to our quiet, painfully shy Joan. In that moment she couldn't help but fall for this long-haired surfer looking boy from Key West, Florida.

Two-months later they were married in the little country church Joan had grown up in. Her faithful dad unsure of this smooth-talking boy, but smart enough to know he couldn't fight it. His daughter had made up her mind and she already belonged to this fella who came out of no where to whisk his fairly naïve daughter off into the sunset.

And these two young love-birds did ride off into that sunset with heads full of hopes and dreams streaming behind them. That twenty-one-year old boy had been around enough to know he had found his excellent wife. Joan was a jewel. His heart was safe in her hands. And for the next nineteen years it was. She would be the rock by his side every step of the way.

Starting out they had nothing. And I mean, *nothing.* But, that didn't slow them down. Tom was the ultimate dreamer and Joan was smart and resourceful. They made the perfect team.

On a tiny plot of land Tom had bought down in the middle of nowhere, they put two old metal buildings together to make a type of dwelling place. Tom wanted peace and solitude, compared to his years of wandering around the country and living in big cities. Joan was raised to be a country girl and felt right at home in their chosen seclusion from the hustle and bustle of big city life. And so, their journey as husband and wife began. Hidden away, invisible to the outside world, lost deep in the hills where the Tennessee, Georgia and North Carolina state lines meet.

Life was tough for these newly-weds. There was no running water in the metal shack they called home, so they had to lug whatever was needed up from the spring that was a good hike from the homesite down a mountain and back up again. This L-shaped shack they 'built' had a pitiful sagging front porch that led to a doorway that you had to stoop down to get in to. The first room was a small corner 'kitchen' simply boasting a long, deep porcelain sink, a small stove, a table that was really just a piece of plywood perched on top of two-by-fours and a giant, old, rusted refrigerator someone had painted blue. That giant, old thing rattled so loudly Tommy was forced to cut it off each night so they could sleep. Young Joan had by no means married into a glamorous lifestyle.

In the summer their metal building was a sauna and in the winter an icebox. Their couch was an old salvaged school bus bench. The tiny bathroom, that never actually worked because there was no indoor plumbing, was used as a closet. At one point they tried to hand-dig a well, until they realized the ridiculousness of their efforts. They tried raising rabbits for meat, but neither of them could stomach the butchering. And so, they learned to live mostly on what they could grow in their small garden patch.

Those early years were hard. But, good. Tom and Joan loved each other deeply as they slowly got to know one another. Two strangers, sharing a life.

As the months turned to years they continued to work hard. Joan's resourcefulness would pay off, as would Tom's risk-taking. Eventually they were able to start their own construction company and bought a larger plot of land with an actual house on it. Though the house was tiny and very, very old. The ultimate 'fixer-upper.' It was a step up from the metal building at least. Still no running water. Still in the middle of nowhere.

Through it all this excellent wife never complained. She worked. She saved. She smiled and laughed. Her husband had no 'lack of gain' thanks to Joan and her willingness to be whatever he needed her to be.

When he needed her to come to work with him in their growing business she didn't hesitate. Though her heart's longing was only to be a mother. She did whatever he asked. When this painfully shy girl was asked to get her real estate license she did so with a smile. She went to work in that office they had built and made herself an asset. She came out of her shell and learned to be an excellent communicator, because her husband needed her to. The office staff and hired workers were all impressed with this excellent wife who exhibited tireless patience. Her gentle spirit and kind ways won everyone over the instant they met her. Tom's success was indeed spurred on by his wife's excellence.

In the late 1970s and early 1980s, it was nearly impossible to give property away, let alone sell it. Tommy began making ends meet by selling marijuana here and there to feed his growing family during the winter months, the slowest time for the real estate market. He passionately believed marijuana should be legalized and would plead his case with any willing ear;

looking back he was truly a man before his time in his beliefs on the drug.

Unfortunately, it would be his passion on this particular subject that would eventually lead to his downfall.

Joan stood apart from her husband on this one thing, knowing it would do more harm to their family than good. Tommy would not listen to his excellent wife. It wasn't until after he was arrested that he realized his mistake of neglecting his family. Though he was never sorry for using and selling the drug, his beliefs set in stone, he did regret not being the husband and father his faithful family deserved him to be. But, the damage was done. His enemies were made. And it was only a matter of time before his past caught up with him.

Through it all Joan would continue to stand by him faithfully, always speaking truth to him and genuinely trying to do what was right.

It reminds me of the story of Nabal and Abigail in the bible. Women often ask the question of what to do when our husbands are not the men of God they are called to be. Women want to know what to do. How to behave in the face of having to still be married to someone who is making bad decisions. Joan did not know what the future would hold when she gave her heart to this man. None of us do. Sometimes things go dreadfully wrong. And, that is where an excellent wife really shines.

There was a man named Nabal who was married to a woman named Abigail. David, who was running from King Saul at the time, went to Nabal for help. Scripture tells us the story of this couple and it is a beautiful picture of an excellent wife living out her faith when her husband is making poor decisions.

"Now the name of the man was Nabal, and the name of his wife Abigail. The woman was discerning and beautiful, but the man was harsh and badly behaved…" (1 Samuel 25:3)

The story goes on to tell us how David had dealt kindly with this man and expected favor in return. But, Nabal lived up to his name, which literally means 'fool.' Because of his folly David sent men to kill Nabal and all his household. When his excellent wife, Abigail, found out about David's plan, scripture says she "made haste and took two hundred loaves and two skins of wine and five sheep already prepared and [about seven quarts] of parched grain and a hundred clusters of raisins and two hundred cakes of figs, and laid them on donkeys. And she said to her young men, 'Go on before me; behold, I come after you.' But she did not tell her husband Nabal. And as she rode on the donkey and came down under cover of the mountain, behold, David and his men came down toward her, and she met them.' (1 Samuel 25:18-20)

As she gave David and his men her beautiful peace offering she also made a most eloquent speech that could only come from an incredibly intelligent and wise woman. Her actions and words saved her and her household from David's wrath.

"Then David received from her hand what she had brought him. And he said to her, 'Go up in peace to your house. See, I have obeyed your voice, and I have granted your petition.' And Abigail came to Nabal, and behold, he was holding a feast in his house like the feast of a king. And Nabal's heart was merry within him, for he was very drunk. So, she told him nothing at all until the morning light. In the morning, when the wine had gone out of Nabal, his wife told him these things, and his heart died within him, and he became as a stone. And about ten days later the LORD struck Nabal, and he died." (1 Samuel 25:35-38)

After the death of Nabal scripture goes on to tell us how David comes back for this excellent wife, now widowed, and makes her his own bride. In our modern culture that may not sound like a storybook ending for Abigail, but in so much of scripture King David symbolizes the true King, that is Christ. This story is a perfect representation of a faithful wife being taken care of by the Savior. Her wisdom and faithfulness are so beautiful. There is so much we can learn from Abigail. Her husband's folly was not her downfall.

That was not the end of *her story*.

Notice she never nagged her husband or spoke down to him. She was simply shrewd when she needed to be and then was honest about it with her husband. She picked her timing wisely. When he was drunk she did not bother. When he was sober and clear-headed she spoke truth in his ear with kindness and gentleness. The truth itself hard enough to hear.

My mom is a woman like Abigail. When her husband began to fall down the downward spiral of his own folly, she spoke truth in his ear. She continued to be his excellent wife to the very end.

And when his end came, she kept on being his excellent wife. All the days of her life she would continue to live up to doing him good and not harm in a myriad of ways. Always faithful. Unwavering. Unnoticed by most. Yet, pointed out and praised by Jesus Himself.

Chapter 3:

Willing Hands

She seeks wool and flax,
and works with willing hands.

She is like the ships of the merchant;
she brings her food from afar.

She rises while it is yet night
and provides food for her household
and portions for her maidens.
Proverbs 31:14-15

My siblings and I laugh good naturedly at our mom's frugalness. For as long as any of us can remember we saw how our mom saved every penny so that we could be taken care of. She once bought a case of black-eyed peas from a hole-in-the-wall saver store only to get them home and discover one of the cans was empty. The next time she visited that store she had her can and receipt with her and demanded they give her a refund of ten cents. We laughed ourselves silly over that one. I can remember the hilariously outraged look in my mother's eyes when she discovered the empty can while she was making us dinner. We tried to tell her not to worry about it, but we knew she wouldn't let it go.

And, essentially that is how we survived after daddy was gone. It wasn't because some magically wealthy person came to our rescue. It was because mom showed prudence when we needed it the most. That is her default. She knows what it is like to not know where your next meal is coming from. She knows the value in counting every bean, every cent, every dollar. As her children, we could rest in that.

In the years after the death of Tommy there was real struggle. For nearly a decade after he was murdered we kids were really too young to help her at all. We looked to her for everything. All our needs were met by her. For nearly a decade she scrimped and saved and worked in her struggling office with willing hands. The 1990s were bleak years for Joan and her little orphans. It wasn't until the turn of the century, when the real estate market picked up, that her business finally started coming out of the ashes. But, during the drought she never gave up. Always hoping for a better day and taking care of us when we couldn't take care of ourselves.

The years were hard for Joan and her children. Though, she was still only in her 30s when she was widowed, she had no parents or grandparents who could come to her aid. They were all gone, except Joan's mentally-ill mother who was like another child to take care of. The years would be unbearably difficult for our young widow and her children.

But, to outsiders it looked like we were fine because of mom's hard work and foresight. And for the most part, we were fine. Somehow, we always had food on the table. Somehow, we always had clothes to wear. As a child I never worried. Though I was smart enough to not ask for much because I knew my mom's pockets were dangerously thin. Yet she worked with willing hands. I never heard her complaints. I never saw her give up. She was never the victim she could have been.

When the real estate/construction business she and daddy had built crumbled around her after his death, she didn't just lie down and die with him and it. She restructured it to suit her strengths and built it back herself. There were many years when she was standing in that office alone. The solo entrepreneur holding up the four walls around her. We kids just played in the back, while she worked in the front. Standing on her own two feet, fighting for everything that we held dear.

When the house she and daddy had built began to crumble around us, she found a way to build it bigger and better. She even paid to bring giant power poles down our forgotten road so we could step into the 21st century, or rather the 20th century! While daddy was alive she had made it work living without electricity. But, now she had to leave us kids alone for too many hours in the day and night while she worked around the clock to feed us. She wanted us to be safe and warm when we came home from school. She wanted us to be comfortable though she couldn't be with us as much. Everything she did was for us.

When Christmas was too sad, she loaded us up and headed to south Florida so we could be with daddy's extended family. She kept us close to them because she knew it was best for us. As we grew and learned to be comfortable with our broken family, she made sure we each had a plethora of gifts under the tree. In her saving she managed to have a yearly Christmas fund set aside just so we could have a merry holiday. I can only remember Christmases of plenty, because mom knew to plan ahead.

When she couldn't come to my away basketball games, I knew it was because she was working and taking care of my younger siblings and anyone else who needed to be taken care of. But, she never missed my home games. I couldn't help but smile as I heard her voice above everyone else's cheering me on. My biggest fan. The loudest cheerleader in my life always pushing me forward.

I'm not sure when she slept. Her energy seemed limitless. And yet, when we begged her to sit with us and watch a movie late at night we noticed she was asleep before it even started. If she ever allowed herself to stop, the weariness of it all would quickly catch her.

Years and years passed as my mom continued to work with her willing hands. Taking each day as it came. Her philosophy always steady. Simply focus on the day at hand. Today is what God has given us and it's our job to see it through.

Joan never allowed herself to be crushed by the burden she had to bear. The cross she was allotted to carry.

I think of her as the little boy willing to share his little bit of fish and bread with thousands of hungry people. Not thinking of the magnitude of his actions. Simply handing it over with a pure, child-like faith that is so precious in the sight of God.

One of his disciples, Andrew,
Simon Peter's brother, said to him,

"There is a boy here
who has five barley loaves and two fish,
but what are they for so many?"

Jesus said,
"Have the people sit down."

Now there was much grass in the place.
So, the men sat down,
about five thousand in number.

Jesus took the loaves,
and when he had given thanks,
he distributed them
to those who were seated.

So also, the fish, as much as they wanted.

And when they had eaten their fill,
he told his disciples,

"Gather up the leftover fragments,
that nothing may be lost."

So, they gathered them up
and filled twelve baskets with fragments
from the five barely loaves
left by those who had eaten.
John 6:8-13

Joan simply gave what she had. All that she had. Which wasn't much. But, it was always more than enough. And as God multiplied what she had given, she dutifully gathered up the fragments so that nothing would be wasted.

As she worked with her willing hands, her household was provided for. She kept us together and held us close. We watched her always. Knowing the jewel that she was. Knowing her strength. My older sisters and I were like her 'maidens' in waiting and she did indeed 'rise while it was yet night' to give us our portions. I can remember explicitly my eldest sister stumbling out of her bedroom one morning as mom merrily went about her business in the kitchen.

"Where is breakfast?" she wanted to know, "Isn't there anything left?"

"You snooze, you lose." Replied our mother, flashing her bright smile and speaking with her gentle voice that was as sweet as an angel's.

In her hard work and gentle ways, she taught us kids what it was to not expect handouts. To not sleep late and then think someone would be there to shelter us. She showed us what it looked like to graciously accept help when it was given, but to ultimately work as hard as we could to never expect or even really need help.

Joan stood alone and showed us how to live on our own two feet. And that was her ultimate motto. This woman who always worked with willing hands and a radiant smile on her face. This woman who never gave up.

We never went without because of her.

After school we would walk into a humble but very comfortable home. The house was empty of our parents' physical presence during those long, early years of drought. But, because of mom, we had a home. Filled with pictures and memories, helping us, guiding us, making sure we knew we were loved and not forgotten.

Though we didn't see her much during those early years, we knew where she was. She was working with willing hands. Smiling in the middle of her sorrow because we all needed her. Taking each day as it came. Falling back to her earliest roots and teachings from her own faithful and hard-working dad who lived off the land.

Simply focus on the task at hand
while taking great comfort in the God who sees.

Though her struggle was great, because she was simply willing to work and give all she had to the Lord, I have no memory of being hungry or in want of anything. She kept a roof over our heads that was warm and comfortable. She kept food in the cupboards that was nourishing and edible. She kept plenty of clothes for us to wear, thanks to her skill of shopping for bargains.

We were well taken care of by our widow mother. The poor widow, working with willing hands simply giving us everything she had. Even all she had to live on.

Chapter 4:

The Business Woman

She considers a field and buys it;
with the fruit of her hands she plants a vineyard.
She dresses herself with strength
and makes her arms strong.

She perceives that her merchandise is profitable.
Her lamp does not go out at night.
She puts her hands to the distaff,
and her hands hold the spindle.
Proverbs 31:16-19

I can see this woman clearly. This woman who is pure muscle from years of hard work and carrying babies on her hip. This woman who cultivates her garden and isn't afraid of dirt and sweat. This woman that is my mom. Joan. The business woman.

Today Joan continues to run her successful real estate business that has been in the same location for forty years. Forty years she has stood strong and weathered the changing tides. Forty years she has seen the ebb and flow of unsteady markets and stood strong as they crashed around her. When others went floating by, she stood firm. Her feet were sure. Set firmly on the Rock Himself.

'Everyone then who hears
these words of mine
and does them
will be like a wise man
who built his house on the rock.

And the rain fell,

and the floods came,

and the winds blew

and beat on that house,

but it did not fall,

because it had been

founded on the rock."

Matthew 7:24-25

Joan stood on the only solid foundation she knew in the months and years following Tommy's death. And that foundation proved true.

When Tom and Joan had first opened their construction business in the early 1970s it wasn't easy. But they persevered and a few years after would also incorporate into a full-fledged real estate firm. Building mountain homes for others who were also trying to escape the hustle and bustle of big city living became their passion. The surrounding mountains, lakes, rivers, and streams seemed to go on forever, sprawling out from their office location. It was an outdoorsman's paradise. And these two young entrepreneurs were adamant to preserve it.

Anyone who worked for them knew it was imperative to save as many trees as possible when putting in a new homesite. They would even build large decks around existing trees instead of cutting them down. Tom and Joan were the ultimate environmentalists. Growing up in Key West allowed Tom to know the gem he had found in these majestic southern Appalachian Mountains that had become his home.

During this time the young couple were also able to build a newer home for their growing family. It was a small cabin simply boasting a tiny kitchen, foyer, eating/reclining area, bathroom and an open concept upstairs for sleeping. As the years went by and their family grew they would add a room on here and there; earning the once tiny house the nickname as the 'patchwork' house. This little home built down in the holler, away from the wind. In today's world they could have built high on the back of their property and carved out a million-dollar lakeview. But, back then that just wasn't the priority. Back then, for them at least, it was more about being smart with where you built and blending in with the surroundings. They believed in making the smallest foot-print possible in order to preserve the picturesque place they called home.

As the years flew by Tom and Joan continued to persevere and weather the ups and downs of their business ventures. The 1980s proved incredibly hard and money was always a fleeting prize to be won. As Tom stumbled and fell into drug-trafficking trying to keep it all together, Joan stood in that office and kept it going. When Tom was arrested, it was Joan, with her baby boy on her hip, standing there holding the walls in place. No matter what, she never let the business go. She knew it was the livelihood that would keep them going even in the face of hardship.

The late 1980s would prove harder than ever for Joan. Living through her husband's arrest, seeing him have to testify to put the bigger catch behind bars, and then being left alone completely as the young widow to a murdered husband in 1991. The storm was great. The waves crashed down one after the other with unrelenting force.

As office employees would quit one by one in the aftermath of Tommy's murder, Joan would stand firm. When Joan was completely alone in her office, she knew the God of the universe could still see her. When we kids were too young to help, Joan dressed herself with strength and kept us alive.

The years continued to beat on us. To beat on Joan. But, she stood firm because of where she stood. Looking back today, she can't even explain how we survived. How we managed to stay afloat in the face of such hardship. The only explanation is that God was with us. Her only answer to this day, is that she simply had faith that God Himself would take care of her and us. Each day she woke with His renewed strength. Each painful moment she carried on as He pulled her through the storm. She would smile as the sun would rise anew. Knowing He was with her.

In Psalm 68 we are given a glimpse of God's heart concerning widows and orphans, when David says these beautiful words:

"Sing to God, sing praises to his name;
lift up a song to him who rides through the deserts;
his name is the LORD; exult before him!

Father of the fatherless and protector of widows
is God in his holy habitation.

God settles the solitary in a home;
he leads out the prisoners to prosperity,
but the rebellious dwell in a parched land."
Psalm 68:4-6

During the years of struggle my mother would work her hands to the bone. She would keep her struggling business going so that her children could eat and live. And we watched God bless her for it. Jesus pointed her out and commended her. The world would ignore us in those early years. But God was with us. Defending us. Caring for us. Holding Joan by the hand, leading her through the storm, protecting her.

***

I still love to visit my mother's house. The house we grew up in. The same house where my dad was murdered at the bottom of the long, winding driveway. The old, now rusted, red gate still in its place as a forever reminder of our very real tragedy. When others would beg us to leave and start a new life, mom knew it was best to stay put. To face the pain and then learn how to carry on. My mother has never run away from a problem. She is slow and thoughtful. Full of wisdom that outsiders can only begin to try and see. We are blessed because we have seen it all.

I love to walk outside in the sprawling woods surrounding the home she built for us. The same woods where hired hitmen sat and watched us for weeks, planning their murderous vengeance on my thirty-nine-year-old father.

I love these woods still, because my mom has sown beauty there. Her organic gardens intricately woven into the natural décor of the property itself. She finds joy in her work. Both in the business world and in her home. And it shows for those of us who have watched her all these years. When others look and can only see her success, I know the deeper story. The story of heart-ache and mistakes. Failure and tears. Nothing was handed to Joan. She is the hardest working woman I've ever known.

Joan, the widow who is my hero, has always lived her life in a manner pleasing to God. Despite any mistakes. I've seen her stumble, but only for a moment before brushing herself off and carrying on, stronger than ever. That is the life of the faithful widow Jesus noticed in the temple. That is the life I've witnessed my mother lead.

A life marked by love, not hate. A life filled with forgiveness, not bitterness. A life of hard work, not laziness. A life ringing with joy and laughter, right along with the tears and mistakes. This accomplished business woman. The hidden woman who taught us what a life ought to be.

Now concerning brotherly love,

you have no need for anyone to write to you,

for you yourselves have been taught by God

to love one another,

for that indeed is what you are doing
to all the brothers throughout [the region].

But we urge you, brothers,
to do this more and more,

and to aspire to live quietly,
and to mind your own affairs,
and to work with your hands,
as we instructed you,

so that you may walk properly before outsiders
and be dependent on no one.

1 Thessalonians 4:9-12

Though scripture often talks of taking care of widows and orphans in their distress, Joan did not sit around and wait for those shining specimens to show up. Ultimately, they didn't. Instead, Joan simply put her faith in the One Person she knew would not let her down. And He took care of us. He protected Joan in her business dealings and allowed her to work quietly with her own hands and mind her own affairs, so that we weren't dependent on anyone.

That old, musty real estate office is forever etched in my memory. The funny looking plaid patent leather couches. The dark brown décor that was so popular in the eighties. The panel walls. The giant topography maps lining those brown walls to show newcomers the way to hidden gems before the internet introduced mapping apps. The framed pictures of roaring white waterfalls that we could lead them to, if only they were adventurous enough to take off their city shoes and let their hair down. It was fun witnessing them fall in love with the mountains we called home.

As very few customers would trickle into our humble, broken down, but very loved office, my mom would treat each one with the utmost care. Her honesty, integrity and experience would win them over one by one. Every dollar she made to keep us alive was made with sheer business savvy and know-how.

I've often heard others say misguided things regarding my mother and her successes. And we just laugh. How can anyone really know unless they lived through each moment as we did?

We know the truth of the matter. And the truth is simply that Joan is the heroine of her own story. God protected her and gave her a way to survive. Joan rose to the occasion without complaint. Without feeling sorry for herself. She took each day as it came and worked with what little she had, knowing God would bless her efforts, in this life or the next. She would not go unnoticed forever.

This incredible business woman. Working diligently each day. Knowing the God of the universe, who sees all, was with her. Faithfully holding her hand on every uphill-step she faithfully climbed. With a forever smile on her lovely, youthful, shining face. Our radiant heroine. Our Joan.

Chapter 5: The Generous Giver

She opens her hands to the poor
and reaches out her hands to the needy.
Proverbs 31:20

My parents were always generous toward others. I have many memories of seeing them helping those in need, expecting nothing in return. And after daddy's death, I witnessed my widowed mom continue walking down the path of selfless generosity.

As a child I watched the people who came in to my mom's humble office to ask her for money. And I watched as my faithful mother always gave to them.

When we sat in church and the offering plate was passed around I saw the large amount she would write on her check with wide eyes. From my point of view, I thought it should be the other way around. Compared to other kids in school we didn't have anything. I wore hand-me-down clothes and my shoes were falling apart. On the rare occasion mom would take me to the store to buy new shoes she always made me buy two sizes too big so they could be worn for as long as possible.

When it came to our daily living mom kept a close eye on all expenses. If clothes were not filthy she would not waste water to clean them. They could be worn again. If we were hungry she would point out that there was a bag of potatoes in the cupboard that were perfectly edible. Or, if no potatoes, then a can of beans. We were never starving. But, we lived very simply thanks to her prudence and patience with us.

Yet, when it came to helping others, Mom was the first to give. And she gave joyfully, expecting nothing in return.

I often picture her with her hands held out, fingers spread wide and straight, as God pours His blessings over them. There is barely anything left on her open palms because His blessings have poured through her fingers to everyone around her. Joan has always been the most generous giver. Even when there really wasn't anything to give, she still gave. Like the widow in the temple who gave it all. That was and is my mom…

Joan: The Cheerful Giver.

The point is this:
whoever sows sparingly
will also reap sparingly,
and whoever sows bountifully
will also reap bountifully.

Each one must give as he has
decided to do in his heart,
not reluctantly or under compulsion,

for God loves a cheerful giver.

And God is able to make all grace abound to you,
so that having all sufficiency
in all things at all times,
you may abound in every good work.

As it is written,

"He has distributed freely,
he has given to the poor;
his righteousness endures forever."

He who supplies

seed to the sower

and bread for food

will supply and multiply

your seed for sowing

and increase the harvest

of your righteousness.

You will be enriched in every way

to be generous in every way,

which through us will produce

thanksgiving to God.

2 Corinthians 9:6-11

Mom never boasted about her giving. Or even said a word about it really. We simply saw it. We still see it. Some people give out of compulsion. Some give when they think others are looking. Joan gives freely, grounded in joy, that can only come from the Father who gives freely to His children. As the widow in the temple knew God saw her as she gave, so my mom gives in secret, knowing her reward from the Father will be great. And it's not in the way you would think.

The 'Prosperity Gospel' in this country would say to give and you can expect a financial return on your investment. God's Word says it is better to give than receive. Give, expecting nothing in return. Give because we are filled with His compassion for others. Give freely, as He freely gave us His only son.

And there lies the secret to being
a genuinely cheerful giver…

In the giving we are blessed. In the giving we know we worship a God who sees. We know all we have essentially has come from Him. It's not ours to keep or give away at all. It's His and we are simply stewards managing His accounts until His return.

Joan gave when times were unbearably hard, because she knew Jesus was with her, providing for her every need.

An old pastor friend of mine used to joke with his congregation and say, "Well, God gave me a good lunch today, but who knows if He'll give me dinner."

Too often our mindset is like this. Being fully satisfied, and yet wondering if God will continue to provide. I watched my mom model for us what it looks like to be a cheerful, generous giver. Not for human praise. But, simply because she believed God loved her and faithfully was watching out for her. As she blessed those around her, He blessed her more still. And the more He blessed, the more she gave. Whatever she had. Time, money, talent, or simply her love. She gave it all freely, expecting nothing in return.

When others hold tight to what they have been given, afraid of what tomorrow might bring, I see my mom faithfully understanding what a vapor this life really is. Her wealth is being stored for her in Heaven. Jesus taught this when He walked the earth. This idea of trusting God each day, instead of trusting our bank accounts and our Americanized perceptions of Christianity. The parable of the rich young fool sums this concept up beautifully in the gospel of Luke.

And [Jesus] said to them,
"Take care, and be on your guard against all covetousness,
for one's life does not consist in the abundance of his possessions."

And he told them a parable, saying,
"The land of a rich man produced plentifully,
and he thought to himself,
'What shall I do, for I have nowhere to store my crops?'

And he said, 'I will do this:
I will tear down my barns and build larger ones,
and there I will store all my grain and my goods.

And I will say to my soul,

"Soul, you have ample goods laid up for many years;
relax, eat, drink, be merry.'"

But God said to him,
'Fool! This night your soul is required of you,
and the things you have prepared, whose will they be?'

So is the one who lays up treasure for himself
and is not rich toward God."
Luke 12:15-21

My mom. The cheerful giver. Not hoarding her possessions to herself. But, blessing everyone around her. Her closet is full of clothes with tags still on them, and so, to the untrained eye she looks to be incredibly wealthy and possessing too much stuff. But, this frugal shopper has found bargains she couldn't pass up, knowing there may be rainy days ahead and inviting anyone in need to come 'shop' in her closet. The 'shopping' is free of course. Always freely giving what she has to those around her. And yet, her smile is more radiant than most.

Her secret is knowing it really is better to give than to receive.

Today I continue to marvel at her generous spirit. When strangers, acquaintances, old friends and family alike all come to her with their hands out, wanting what she has, she gives freely still. They don't know that she is not giving out of her abundance, but that she is giving literally all she has. Though the untrained eye cannot see it. The untrained eye scoffs at her success and assumes wrongful thoughts.

As her blessed daughter, I see it clearly. But, more importantly, Joan, our cheerful giver, knows Someone else is watching and noticing…

Jesus, God wrapped in flesh, sees her.

He saw her as a little girl growing up on a farm in the dusty hills of north Georgia. A puny little thing with a mentally-ill mother unable to care for her, a father who was forced to practically work himself to death, and two younger siblings that she was responsible to care for. Joan. Our little heroine who loved God with all she had.

God also saw her when she was swept away by her rolling-stone of a husband into her very non-glamorous kind of life. Bare-foot and pregnant without the simple comforts of running water and electricity.

God saw her when she took care of her father-in-law and his brother who were wasting away from alcoholism. God saw her when her husband's mistakes weighed heavy and she thought she would break under the pressure. But, He held her up and she kept going.

When Joan's own father died unexpectedly from a stroke when she was only twenty-eight-years-old and pregnant with her third child, God saw her lovingly take in her twelve-year-old sister to raise as her own. He saw her as she faithfully took care of an aging mother diagnosed with Paranoid Schizophrenia and an aging brother with the same mental illness. As her brother bounced around the prison system for too many years, it would be Joan who fought for him. Not backing down until his illness was properly diagnosed and she could bring him home to care for him. She would also be the one caring for her mom, who had the mind of two-year-old, as she withered away from Pancreatic Cancer. Joan would never leave her dying mother's side. Our beautiful heroine always taking care of hers.

God saw her as she stood by her husband's side, loving him and supporting him to the very end. Joan. Our excellent wife that is far more precious than jewels.

He saw her taking care of her young children when they were left fatherless and alone. Joan. Our young widow with the quiet strength that never went unnoticed by Jesus. He knew her story. And, He knew, as He was sitting in the temple that day pointing her out to His disciples, that it was His Father, God Himself, who protected this faithful widow.

Whoever is generous to the poor lends to the LORD,
and he will repay him for his deed.
Proverbs 19:17

I can't help but think how Jesus called her the 'poor widow' and yet didn't stop her from putting in all she had to live on into that offering box. He allowed her to give it all away. As you read in the book of Mark there is just this picture of Jesus sitting there, allowing this dreadfully, pitifully poor, lonely widow to give away all she had. This concept is so outrageously foreign to me as I ponder it. This concept is so foreign to most American Christians today. We only know how to give out of our abundance. Few of us have ever faced real poverty. Yet, that is one of the sparkles in Joan's beautiful, clear blue eyes.

She has lived in poverty. The kind of poverty where she really didn't know where her next meal was coming from. And though we can argue about who is the poorest of the poor in third world countries from now until the end of time, I don't want you to miss this truth. If you have ever been truly hungry. Truly out of money. With no where to turn. Then you know what Joan has lived through.

There were times in her life when things were so hard that yes, she was that incredibly poor widow. And yet, into that temple she walked, eagerly dropping in everything she had to live on. Trusting her life to the only One who could truly save her.

After living through that, and coming through it, there is no way to fully explain the blessing of being a generous giver.

"How can Joan be so cheerful and give so much?" I've heard people ask. It's simple really. She has always given. Even when there was nothing to give, she gave with that infamous radiant smile spread across her joyful face. She gave then. She gives still. And she will be forever blessed.

Chapter 6: She Has No Fear

She is not afraid
of snow for her household,

for all her household
are clothed in scarlet
[or in double thickness].

She makes bed coverings for herself;
her clothing is fine linen and purple.
Proverbs 31:21-22

Joan could hear the kids screaming outside as they came running toward the house. Snakes. Everywhere. They had stumbled onto a nest of Copperheads. Without a moment to lose Joan sprang into action. There was no one to call. There was only Joan. Fear was not an option. She ran to her children's aid. On her way she grabbed the one weapon closest to her: a shovel. With shovel firmly in her strong hands she ascended on the snakes, killing them with expert precision.

Her young children watched in horror from the living room window, staring in awe at the woman who was their mother.

Joan didn't have time to be afraid. There were too many people depending on her. Her love was so much stronger than fear. She simply did what had to be done. And her children could take comfort in her faithfulness. Always.

After her husband's murder, Joan and her children didn't go home for months. They slept huddled together in the back of the real estate office.

Not because Joan was afraid, but because her children were. She gave us time to heal. Time to catch our breath.

During those months of hiding she used her resourcefulness to build additional bedrooms on our small home and put in electricity. She did it all for us. So that we could be excited about something. She even let us pick out the décor. The color of the carpet, walls, bed coverings, and so on. No matter how wacky or impractical it was. I was ten and wanted a glistening white and pearl room. She consented to our every wish, no matter how outlandish. She knew I would never be able to keep a glistening white room glistening for long. But, that didn't matter. She knew what she was doing.

When we finally returned home our new bedrooms were waiting for us with actual electric lamps that turned on at the flip of a switch. She knew what we needed in that moment. We desperately needed a distraction before the shock wore off and the pain settled deep into our bones. Over the years the shining bedroom that she built for me became my place of solitude. When she saw me coil inward with my deep thoughts, she gifted me my first journal and encouraged me to write.

Wise Joan was never afraid for her household; she prepared us all for the coming winter snow that she knew we would all have to walk through. The dark places we would wander trying to make sense of the tragedy. She knew we all had to make our peace in our own time. The pain was heavy. But Joan expertly prepared us each in different ways. She knew our individual souls would desperately need healing as we grew. And mom was patient with us as we would stumble and fall. Which we all did. In numerous ways.

But her patience never faltered. She stayed the course even when we were lost in our pain. When we were blind to God's love, mom's faith was stronger still. And though we couldn't see Him, we could always see her. In our darkness she was the light shining the way.

Joan was our model - Jesus was hers

The rumors still soar in our small town about the death of Joan's husband, our beloved daddy, our fun-loving, adventurous Tommy. We've all heard them. How he can't be dead. How he must be in hiding. Still, after nearly thirty years have passed the rumors are stronger than ever. People want to know if he's really gone. When we ask why they think he's still alive the answer never ceases to amaze us:

Because we are all too happy.

How can a widow and her orphaned children be happy? How can they laugh and smile and dance and play in the rain? How can they go on with life like everything is okay?

It just isn't natural.

And the answer is that no, it's not natural. It's supernatural.

Why does the book of James tell us in chapter one verse twenty-seven that '[r]eligion that is pure and undefiled before God, the Father, is this: to visit orphans and widows in their affliction, and to keep oneself unstained from the world[?]'

Because James is giving us a peak into the very heart and mind of our Savior. Jesus said to let the little children come to Him. And when our dad was wrongfully ripped away from us, we ran into the arms of our Heavenly Father, thanks to our mom. She pointed the way, knowing He alone would heal our gaping wounds.

God does take care of the widows and orphans. Joan and her children are living proof of His promise and faithfulness. When the world would laugh and scoff at us, or simply forget us, God held us up. When our pain was great and we stumbled into the darkness, God would use our dear widowed mother to shine the light so we could see.

I love what He says in scripture concerning widow's and orphans. Looking back, I know His Love surrounded us, despite the darkness we were lost in.

Scripture is full of beautiful insights of how our awesome Creator thinks of widows and orphans.

Wash yourselves;
make yourselves clean;
remove the evil of your deeds
from before my eyes;
cease to do evil,
learn to do good;
seek justice, correct oppression;

bring justice to the fatherless,
plead the widow's cause.

Isaiah 1:16-17

You shall not mistreat

any widow or fatherless child.

If you do mistreat them,

and they cry out to me,

I will surely hear their cry…

Exodus 22:22-23

'Cursed be anyone

who perverts the justice due to the sojourner,

the fatherless, and the widow.'

And all the people shall say, 'Amen.'

Deuteronomy 27:19

The LORD watches

over the sojourners;

he upholds the widow

and the fatherless,

but the way of the wicked

he brings to ruin.

Psalm 146:9

Joan will be the first to say that it was the LORD watching over her during the years following her untimely widowhood. Though her fear should have been great, she was not afraid. Though we should have perished right along with our dad, we survived. Though the years of struggle should have destroyed us, we came out on the other side refined like gold. We passed through the fire and lived to tell the tale. Not because we are perfect. Not because Joan is perfect, she made plenty of mistakes that we will get to, but because God is perfect. And our perfect God cares for His widows and orphans and commands His people to do the same.

Today when you see Joan around town you can never guess that she is that poor widow Jesus points out to us. She just doesn't fit the mold of what people picture a poor widow looking like. Her looks are still youthful because she is young at heart. Her joyfulness radiates out of her permanent white smile. Her eyes full of genuine laughter.

My own husband still points out that she is the best dressed woman in town. And if you comment to her about her perfectly matching outfit, she will boast in the fact that it cost her usually no more than two or three dollars. I love to hear her laugh as she tells me her shirt only cost a quarter. She is a frugal shopper, but you would never know. She is dressing herself still in 'fine linen and purple' with the same tight budget she has always had.

Her worth is more than the average stranger could possibly comprehend. More than diamonds and gold and rubies and jewels. Her worth is far more precious and hidden in the heart. We are the lucky ones who know her worth. Joan. The woman with absolutely no fear. The hidden widow. Our little heroine who is still as 'God-loving' as ever.

Chapter 7:

Unlucky in Love

Her husband is known in the gates
when he sits among the elders of the land.
Proverbs 31:23

Her late husband, Tommy, is definitely 'known in the gates,' not only because of what happened to him, but because of his wife's faithfulness, just as scripture promises. He found an excellent wife in Joan, our beautiful God-loving heroine. And she has done him good and not harm all her life.

When misinformed strangers and acquaintances wrongly conclude that her joyful attitude can only mean that she never really was a poor widow, how I wish they could know the hard, ugly truth. The truth that this amazing woman really is as amazing as she appears. There are no gimmicks. No dirty parlor tricks. Her husband of nineteen years, the love of her youth, really was murdered in cold blood on that horrific October morning all those years ago. Anyone who says otherwise is grasping at air. Trying to take the spotlight off the cold, hard truth that is his unsolved murder.

And so, young Joan was alone. Truly alone. Except for a house full of children. Bills to be paid. A business to rebuild. There was nothing but heart-ache and a bleak future to look forward to. Who would marry a woman with no prospects? A woman with a million crazy kids to take care of? A woman with an elderly mother out of her mind hanging around causing chaos? A woman with a brother in and out of prison, suffering from an undiagnosed mental illness, constantly causing trouble? A woman with a home falling apart? Broken in so many ways. Seemingly beyond repair.

Joan was beautiful. And smart. Not yet forty-years-old. She was the young widow scripture tells to remarry.

So, I would have younger widows marry,
bear children, manage their households,
and give the adversary no occasion for slander.
1 Timothy 5:14

It wasn't that Joan completely disregarded this command. Our young widow may have never remarried, but not for lack of trying on her part.

Though young Joan was completely caught up in the chaos of everyday survival, she still felt the loneliness. She had been married longer than she had been single. She had married Tommy at the age of eighteen and was with him for nineteen years. It was impossible to completely close herself off to the hope of finding love again. At thirty-seven she still had so many years ahead. As we see in scripture, God would rather a young widow marry. God knows us so well. When a young woman is used to being married, He does not expect her to stay alone in her youth.

But, for the next seventeen years Joan would remain a young widow unmarried. Not for lack of trying. Not for lack of character or beauty. On the contrary. Many men would try to woo her over the years, but unfortunately her want-to-be suitors were mostly low lives, for lack of a better phrase. Think about it. Who wants to marry a woman with a house full of crazy kids? And we were crazy. Not because mom was a bad mom, but because she had to be the dad. She had to be our sole provider. She didn't have the luxury of kissing our wounds away, breaking up fights, or making our home tidy and neat. We were in survival mode, and that was a terrifying sight for any young man.

And this is where the enemy caused young Joan to falter. The first man who came along that actually wanted to marry her turned out to be a lunatic, so she sent him packing right away. No harm done.

After that Joan began to get her own feet under her a bit better. And then the real low lives began coming out of the wood work. I watched men who clearly used her for what they could gain from her. Men who had no intention of being a father to her kids. Men who took advantage of our young widow.

And in His teaching, [Jesus] said,

"Beware of the scribes,
who like to walk around in long robes
and like greetings in the marketplaces
and have the best seats in the synagogues

and the places of honor at feasts,

who devour widows' houses

and for a pretense make long prayers.

They will receive the greater condemnation."

Mark 12:38-40

About three years after her husband was gone she began dating one of these 'winning guys' and fell for him, thinking he might be Mr. Right. Unfortunately, Joan became pregnant with her sixth child out of wedlock. Looking back Joan would say this was her lowest point after Tommy's death. She felt desperate to be loved and had fallen far from that faithful girl she had always been. The father to this child quickly ran away scared, not able to handle the magnitude of the responsibility.

So, there Joan stood. Alone again. This time with even more children depending on her.

But, here the story is bitter-sweet. Where the enemy thought Joan would falter for good, it was really what caused her stronger resolve. Here her determination and grit would prove to live her life pleasing to the LORD more than ever.

And, the baby?

He was God's gift to our broken, hurting family. Psalm 127:3 says *'[b]ehold, children are a heritage from the LORD, the fruit of the womb a reward. Like arrows in the hand of a warrior are the children of one's youth. Blessed is the man [or woman] who fills his [or her] quiver with them! They shall not be put to shame when they speak with their enemies in the gate.'*

This baby brought laughter and joy that had been missing from our home. This baby multiplied our love ten-fold. He was bright and sweet and funny. And we all fell deeply in love with this little brother, this little gift in a time of darkness.

Joan nursed her babe with raw thankfulness, knowing he would be her very last. This little girl who had grown up always wanting to be a mom. The young widow blessed and seen by her loving Creator.

It would not be easy having yet another mouth to feed over the years. But that would not take away the deep-rooted joy of it all. Children are a blessing from God. No matter the circumstances. No matter what takes place when our loving Heavenly Father expertly knits them together in their mother's womb. Children are His most precious blessings to us.

For you formed my inward parts;
you knitted me together
in my mother's womb,

I praise you,
for I am fearfully
and wonderfully made.

Wonderful are your works;
my soul knows it very well.

My frame was not hidden from you,
when I was being made in secret,
intricately woven in the depths of the earth.

Your eyes saw my unformed substance;
in your book were written,
every one of them,
the days that were formed for me,
when as yet there was none of them.

Psalm 139:13-16

What beautiful scripture. Reminding us of His goodness and mercies. A situation that could have ruined Joan, simply brought her right back to where she belonged. Into the arms of Jesus.

The years continued to stretch on and Joan continued to persevere as she had always done. Among the chaos of little children, a house that was never clean, a business always calling her name, and bills that had to be paid, she continued to trust that God would provide for her family. And, of course, He did.

Finally, after nearly a decade of being a widow, Joan met a most interesting man. He had traveled the world, spoke numerous languages and noticed Joan's radiant smile with a hint of sadness in her eyes. He would be a spark that put glitter in her life. Joan found herself swept away by this foreign man. Her children were finally old enough that she could travel some and actually feel young again.

Eventually the cute, adventurous couple decided that they would marry. This man was kind and unafraid of her growing children. And her children actually liked him. The first they had liked in all the years of possible suitors. Things were seeming to fall in place at last.

But then, tragedy.

A plane crash and another precious life taken. Instead of the wedding we were all hoping for, there was a funeral in its place. The fleeting glimmer of hope for Joan and her kids was gone again. The happiness they had hoped to share, snuffed out in an instant. Again.

This was almost more than they could bear. Everyone who knew Joan best had wanted this for her. If anyone deserved to be happy it was this beautiful, faithful, young widow. Joan was utterly crushed.

But, God was faithful still.

The LORD is near to the brokenhearted
and saves the crushed in spirit.
Psalm 34:18

The grieving process for Joan was different this time. Her children were older now and didn't need her as much as they had. We were all broken as we watched her grieve. The heroine of our story beaten down, possibly down for the count.

But, Joan slowly stood up again. She took a long breath and put one foot in front of the other. We witnessed the same Spirit that kept her going when our dad had been killed, keep her going again. Her faith was stronger than circumstances. Her God bigger than tragedy. And so, she clung to the only thing that she could, the only thing solid enough to stand on. The Rock that is Jesus Christ Himself.

Chapter 8: Strength and Dignity

She makes linen garments and sells them;
she delivers sashes to the merchant.

Strength and dignity are her clothing,
and she laughs at the time to come.
Proverbs 31:24-25

As a child walking through the store lost from mom, I had no worry. I knew I would hear her eventually. That famous laugh of hers. It would ring out above all other noise. I would follow the laughter and find her. My mom's laugh is contagious. It's loud and hearty and incredibly real. And when she is not laughing out loud, her eyes are laughing still.

This woman in Proverbs that 'laughs at the time to come' is most definitely describing our heroine. Our Joan. She laughs because her joy runs deeper than most people could ever imagine. Great pain and grief has led her down the road to even greater joy. She is thankful. And her thankfulness spills overflowingly into her beautiful joyfulness.

Dignity that says she is worthy of honor with pure, raw strength describes Joan well. When she walks into a room, her head is held high, not pridefully, but with pure dignity. When she was voted *Realtor of the Year* by her peers a few years ago she rightfully received a standing ovation. Her genuine look of surprise was adorable. She had spent the last fifteen years as the quiet widow working to take care of her children, running her business with integrity, minding her own affairs. Now as she stood to receive her award, she was surprised that others around her had noticed. They had, of course, noticed. Somehow over the years of struggle Jesus had been pointing her out to others who were willing to look and see.

Her peers were genuinely happy for her to receive an award and give her a deserved standing ovation. Because to know this woman is to fall in love with her, and it's a love that will last a lifetime.

Even still, people want to know how this woman can laugh so joyfully. As much as the standing ovation was a nice moment, it wasn't the prize she had been striving for all those years. It was something much deeper. Something hidden. Something secret. Her striving was never in vain, even if she had never had a standing ovation in a crowded banquet hall, because she had been diligently working day after day, moment by moment, with a smile on her face and deep-rooted joy that is confusing to most.

"No one can be that happy," the nay-sayers say, "No one is naturally that joyful." We hear it all. And we laugh at the confusion. Because we know her well. And, yes. It is positively who she is to her very core. Joan has lived through great tragedy, and come out the other side refined, as the beautiful gem that she has always been. Joan, our God-loving heroine is a beautiful picture for us of what God's joy looks like.

You have turned for me
my mourning into dancing;

you have loosed my sackcloth
and clothed me with gladness,
that my glory may sing your praise
and not be silent.

O LORD my God,
I will give thanks to you forever!

Psalm 30:11-12

When our mom dances people laugh. Not because it is completely embarrassing, but because it is clear that she is dancing for joy. If King David ever needed a dancing partner, my mom would have been perfect. Her joy comes bursting forth and she can not contain it. The nay-sayers stand there gaping, wanting to know where her strong drink is. But, Joan doesn't drink. She is simply full of uncontainable joy.

Then our mouth was filled with laughter,
and our tongue with shouts of joy…
Those who sow in tears
shall reap with shouts of joy!
Psalm 126:2,6

Joan's faith in Christ is the source of her joy. A faith you can see. Bubbling over and flowing out of her for all to behold. When people walk away perplexed, I wish I could get their attention and say, 'Look, can't you see it? Don't you know about the joy we have in Jesus?' That is her joy.

Though her mourning was great, and the sadness is still felt to this day, her joy in Jesus is greater still. Though the tears over these long years have been many, Jesus has bottled them all and says they are precious. Joan sowed in tears as the years beat her down, and the sun would not shine. We watched her closely and wondered what would come of her sowing.

But, it didn't take long for God to immensely bless her sowing; and now we all rejoice with her as she reaps her bountiful harvest with pure, unadulterated shouts of joy.

Blessed be the God and Father

of our Lord Jesus Christ!

According to his great mercy,
he has caused us to be born again
to a living hope through
the resurrection of Jesus Christ from the dead,

to an inheritance that is imperishable,
undefiled, and unfading, kept in heaven for you,
who by God's power are being guarded through faith
for a salvation ready to be revealed in the last time.

In this you rejoice,

though now for a little while, if necessary,
you have been grieved by various trials,

so that the tested genuineness of your faith –
more precious than gold that perishes
though it is tested by fire –

may be found to result in praise and glory and honor
at the revelation of Jesus Christ.

Though you have not seen him, you love him.

Though you do not now see him,

you believe in him

and rejoice with joy that is inexpressible

and filled with glory,

obtaining the outcome of your faith,

the salvation of your souls.

1 Peter 1:3-9

Joan's faith has been tested by horrific trials in this life. Yet, after she walked through the fire, her faith was found to result in praise toward her Heavenly Father. The genuineness of her faith was truly tested. Her smile reveals this great mystery of God. Though we walk through the fire, we are not burned, but refined. When our faith is real, we come out shining even brighter than before.

Though she did not ask to be the young, poor widow; Joan did choose to be the widow in the temple who gave all she had back to the God who had saved her. Giving it all willingly, joyfully, to the God who has always been with her. The God who will never leave her. No matter the pain, no matter the trials, her hope will remain in Him.

Her strength is in Him. And through the years of pain and heart-ache she grew stronger and stronger. She worked harder and harder. Keeping her dignity by never giving up. The road was hard. Harder than most can comprehend. Yet, our heroine stayed steady. She knew Jesus was in the fire with her. Protecting her. Leading her. Fighting for her. Thoughts of revenge have melted away as she knows the God of justice is near to her.

The God who sees.

The God who hears.

This God who is clear about what to do when we are wronged. Though in the immediate aftermath of Tommy's murder her mind was filled with thoughts of revenge, her unwavering faith never faltered and eventually God would gently lead her back into the freedom of forgiveness and peace. Over the years Joan would trust Him in this as well as everything else. Her joy is complete in knowing God has always been in control. Even when her beloved Tommy was murdered in cold blood. God was in control and His Word still stands above all, guiding us when life does not make sense.

Finally, all of you,
have unity of mind, sympathy,

brotherly love, a tender heart,
and a humble mind.

Do not repay evil for evil
or reviling for reviling,

but on the contrary, bless,
for to this you were called,
that you may obtain a blessing.

For "Whoever desires to love life
and see good days,
let him keep his tongue from evil
and his lips from speaking deceit;

let him run away from evil and do good;
let him seek peace and pursue it.

For the eyes of the Lord are on the righteous,
and his ears are open to their prayer.

But the face of the Lord
is against those who do evil."

Now who is there to harm you
if you are zealous for what is good?

But even if you should suffer
for righteousness' sake,
you will be blessed.

Have no fear of them,
nor be troubled, but in your hearts
honor Christ the Lord as holy

always prepared to make a defense
to anyone who asks you
for a reason for the hope that is in you;

yet do it with gentleness and respect,
having a good conscience,
so that, when you are slandered,
those who revile your good behavior in Christ
may be put to shame.

For it is better to suffer for doing good,
if that should be God's will,
than for doing evil.

1 Peter 3:8-17

The hope and the joy found in Joan is indeed because of Christ. Those of us who know her best know this simple truth.

Joan. Living up to her name. Always.

Our beautiful, wonderful God-loving heroine always pointing us back to Him. The God of the universe who can and does turn our mourning into joy, our tears into laughter, and our great trials into a life well lived.

Chapter 9: Sharing Her Gifts

She opens her mouth with wisdom,
and the teaching of kindness is on her tongue.
Proverbs 31:26

Joan leads by example. The perfect teacher for us young women. I am more about words, she is more about doing. And, when I became a married woman with a house full of children of my own, I finally realized what an example she was for me.

One of my favorite books in the bible is Titus. Numerous women's bible studies focus on Titus chapter two where it describes how the older women should teach the younger women. For years I would look around my church diligently, desperately searching for the 'older women' who were suppose to be teaching me. I went to all the ladies' bible studies and attended every women's ministry event I could.

But, it all fell a bit flat. I felt lost in the verbiage and desperately craved someone who could simply come along side me and show me what it was to live out my calling as a young wife and mother.

Then, the lightbulb lit up. Really it crashed into me and finally woke me out of my stupor. I certainly needed a giant knock on the head to do so. How blind I had been. My hard-headed self somehow had missed that I already had the perfect teacher. I just had to go back to that beautiful young widow I knew so well.

Older women likewise
are to be reverent in behavior,
not slanderers or slaves to much wine.

They are to teach what is good,
and so train the young women

to love their husbands and children,
to be self-controlled, pure, working at home,
kind and submissive to their own husbands,
that the word of God may not be reviled.

Titus 2:3-5

First of all, mom lived out what God calls a young woman to do right before my eyes. Before she was a widow, and even afterward. She never stopped loving us. Not for one second. She was always a picture of self-control and purity. Her willing hands never ceased working, day and night, whether in our home or in our family business that daddy had wanted her to work in.

She was always kind, even in the face of great stress. And while still married, she was truly the most excellent wife, submitting to his wishes, yet always standing on truth. When daddy refused to attend church, she would take us herself so we could learn about the man Jesus whom she loved so much. And after daddy's death, she never faltered, still attending the same church all these years later.

The other thing I slowly began to notice as I've been busy raising my own children, is how my mom was a faithful attender and monetary giver to her church, yet she never stood out in the limelight as any type of leader. As a child and young adult, I wrongly assumed it was because she had nothing to offer. No talents to give. Maybe just not enough knowledge to teach or lead a class, women's ministry event, Sunday School program, or Bible School week.

But, boy oh boy, was I so wrong!

As a grandma and empty-nester today, my mom works diligently wherever she is needed in her home church. She teaches young girls' classes and even drives the church bus to pick up impoverished kids so they can have a hot meal on Wednesday nights. They have a ton of kids who show up to their program during the week, all looking for a hot meal and some kind of hope.

My mom. Joan. Is their favorite person. Her love reaches out and they can't get enough.

Her wisdom speaks volumes as I open my eyes to see. Her kindness to the hurting rivals that of any saint. She is a wonder to behold.

Now I see my teacher clearly. Joan. The true God-loving heroine of our story. And she gives me permission to focus on today. To focus on what is right in front of me. When other women at church ask me to add more activities to my calendar, I can say no with a clear conscience. It is not my season for that. It is my season for growing babies, kissing scraped knees, working hard at home, and being my husband's helper in whatever way he needs me. And this season of being at home, that God has given me, is very precious.

Joan has taught me this truth by modeling it for me as my siblings and I were growing up. Not sitting me down and preaching at me, but by simply living out her faith in front of me my whole life.

She does speak wisdom occasionally. And, the teachings of kindness are on her lips through small words here and there. Words are okay for those small teachable moments; actions though, are much louder than words. Joan is a wise, wise woman, and knows this well. It has been her actions that have always pointed the way for any of us who are willing to pay attention.

Jesus pointed to the poor widow in the temple that day, not only to praise her faithfulness, but to teach His disciples. By pointing her out to them in that teachable moment He was essentially saying, 'Look at her. She has it figured out.'

Through her actions, it is crystal clear that Joan has it figured out.

The excellent wife described in Proverbs 31 is a teacher to her children and all who come to know her. Her words are wise and kind. Words of life that uplift and restore. Joan always sees the positive in everyone. She always has hope for their restoration because she knows the One who restores people. I am blessed to have her as my teacher. Modeling the way for me. Even still.

A disciple is not above his teacher,

but everyone when he is fully trained

will be like his teacher.

Luke 6:40

I can only hope to emulate the character of my mom someday. This woman who is so full of faith. So full of joy. Full of kindness and compassion for everyone around her. Touching countless lives for the better. Encouraging. Fearless. Strong and beautiful. Free from any bitterness or hate; but wrapped up completely in perfect Love Himself.

Joan's faith is contagious. Being with her gives you a glimmer of Him. The One true God. The Creator of heaven and earth. The Maker of Joan herself. Jesus. The God-Man who has gifted her this great faith. When you are with her, you can't help but want it. Her smile tells you it's real. Her dancing eyes tell you it's worth it. This forever youthful woman exhibiting her precious child-like faith that is so lovely in the sight of God.

His Word tells us that we cannot enter His kingdom without becoming first like a child. Children run to Joan because they know she is their kindred spirit. Loving Jesus just because. Loving Jesus because she has always done so.

As a child I knew my mom would never let me down. As an adult, I realize it was because she knew her Heavenly Father would never let her down.

As the church bus pulls up to a house with hungry children standing outside waiting to be picked up, the doors open and they see an angel on earth smiling at them. They know they are safe with her. They know she possesses something worth having. They know her life has been hard, too. And she is the brightest thing they have ever seen. So just maybe they will live through their storm, too. Just maybe there is real hope in this broken world. They run to her and hug her. Their hearts bursting with an understanding that she truly cares for them and understands their brokenness.

Then children were brought to him

that he might lay his hands

on them and pray.

The disciples rebuked the people,

but Jesus said,

"Let the little children come to me

and do not hinder them,

for to such belongs the kingdom of heaven."

Matthew 19:13-14

Jesus said to let the children come to Him. Joan is simply showing them the way. Shining the Light onto their dark path and simply loving them in the midst of their pain. The same way she did when her own children were growing up. The same way she does with every single person she meets.

Oh, how we need more people in this broken world like Joan. Shining bright, piercing the darkness, and beautifully reflecting the Son.

Chapter 10: Taking Care of Hers

She looks well to the ways of her household
and does not eat the bread of idleness.
Proverbs 31:27

Joan has always taken care of others. Before she married Tom, at the age of eighteen, she was already accustomed to shouldering the bulk of chores around her childhood home and farmstead because her mother had Paranoid Schizophrenia which grew worse with each passing year. When Joan's baby sister was born she was sixteen-years-old, and Joan assumed responsibility in taking care of the baby because their mom was not well enough to.

Just before Joan graduated high-school, this sad memory is forever etched in her mind. Perhaps it's why her entire family forgot about her eighteenth birthday that particular month of May. At seventeen-years-old Joan would sit on the front porch of her parents' old farmhouse, holding her one-year-old baby sister, tearfully watching the authorities take her mother away. Again. Seeing the terrified look in her mom's eyes as they loaded her in the back of the squad car and driving her down the bumpy dirt road finally to disappear out of sight as they headed toward the asylum. For months at a time Joan's mother would be gone. This unhappy scenario had been an all too frequent occurrence for

Joan throughout her childhood. Because of her mother's illness, young Joan was forced to grow up very quickly.

Then, as a young married woman, it wasn't long before her own children came. Tom was not a hands-on kind of dad when it came to actually helping. He never changed a diaper or stayed up with a screaming baby. He would play with their kids and be a big kid himself, much to his children's delight; but when it came to helping Joan at all, that was out of the question. She did it all from the very beginning.

When Tom's alcoholic dad began to fade, Joan took care of him. When Tom's alcoholic bachelor uncle began to fade, it was Joan who took the time to check-in and help however she could.

She was always looking out for her own just as scripture tells us to. First Timothy chapter five talks about this subject. About taking care of relatives and the clear reprimands for those who don't. It says that 'if anyone does not provide for his relatives, and especially for members of his household, he has denied the faith and is worse than an unbeliever.'

Once again, Joan showed her strong faith by simply taking care of who was right in front of her. Wherever the need arose, she was there with love to give.

When Joan's own father died suddenly from a stroke, she didn't hesitate to take in her twelve-year-old sister to raise and love as her own daughter. From the world's point of view Tom and Joan were crazy to do this. They already had two young daughters of their own and a third one on the way. So, in one year they went from two daughters, to four. Money was tight. But Joan's love was as big as ever.

The years passed and the family grew even bigger. As Joan entered into young widowhood she had more people than ever depending on her. But she stayed strong. Continuing to look to the ways of her own house and not sitting idle allowing herself to be any kind of victim. No matter how hard things became. And the years were hard on her.

I often wonder at the stories my own husband tells me. He works in the insurance industry and it always baffles me when men tell him their wives and children won't need anything after they are gone. They are so stubbornly confident that someone will come along and care for them. But, Joan and her little orphans are living proof that doesn't always happen. If ever.

There were no friends or family members jumping to Joan's rescue in the wake of her tragedies. No one was willing or even able to encompass the magnitude of her dilemma. When asking her today who came to help, her answer is surprisingly sad. She mentions a couple of friends by name who gave her a little money. A hundred dollars here and there in the immediate aftermath. But, as much as those generous givers were greatly appreciated and still remembered, it was merely a drop in the bucket when it came down to it.

And as far as another man coming in to her life and saving her? Not a chance.

Joan was just as beautiful and becoming as the next woman. Marrying her would have been easy enough. We've already shown what an excellent wife she was and is. However, can any stranger really look at a bunch of kids that don't belong to him and just magically want to care for them? Or at a mentally-ill mother-in-law who would dutifully speed-dial the police, making up crazy stories about him, rather than have him walk into their home and marry her daughter?

No, there was no one who came to our rescue. There was no amazing man knocking on our door to take care of us in our distress.

By the time Joan had her sixth child, counting her sister, her seventh, she was also solely responsible for taking care of her elderly, mentally-ill mother who acted more like a two-year-old. There seemed to be no end to the people in Joan's life who needed her. She didn't have time to sit, let alone feel sorry for herself. God was continuing to mold her into who He wanted her to be. Our, beautiful, faithful widow. Giving all to the King.

There are foolish people in our small town who actually tried to say Joan never remarried because our dad was still alive. Simply hiding out somewhere that only we knew about. Because she never remarried and seemed so joyful, they figured this could be the only possibility to the great mystery they were witnessing.

The young, poor widow and her pathetic orphans somehow smiling through their tears. Somehow finding reasons to laugh through their overwhelming sorrow.

But, God Himself tells us to stay joyful through our trials. He walked with Joan, and she walked with us. Living out her great faith in the most beautiful ways.

Count it all joy, my brothers,

when you meet trials of various kinds,

for you know that the testing

of your faith produces steadfastness.

And let steadfastness have its full effect,
that you may be perfect and complete,
lacking in nothing.

If any of you lacks wisdom,
let him ask God,

who gives generously to all
without reproach,
and it will be given him.

But let him ask in faith,
with no doubting,
for the one who doubts
is like a wave of the sea
that is driven and tossed by the wind.

For that person must not suppose
that he will receive anything from the Lord;

he is a double-minded man,
unstable in all his ways.
James 1:2-8

Do we really believe this scripture? The very Word of God. He says that we should be *joyful* when trials come. *Joyful* when life is at its hardest. *Joyful* when the happy storybook ending is not on the horizon.

Joan is joyful in her sorrow. And she has suffered for that, too. The rumors would fly around her for years as she kept her beautiful smile as radiant as ever. She did not doubt God's goodness through the years of drought. And He blessed her immensely for it.

Yes, her business essentially became more successful. But that is not the blessing scripture often speaks of.

God has blessed Joan with unshakable faith.

Yes, faith is a gift from God and a blessing to be treasured. Faith that is tested in the fire and comes out purer than ever before. Faith in a steadfast God while living in a crazy world. Faith that God is still in control and will always be in control. Faith that God knows what is best for us, even when life is hard and does not make any sense.

The world sees Joan's faith, like so many others who have come before her, and scoffs. They don't understand her faith. This blessing God has given her in the midst of her sorrow. This faith that has produced her true joyfulness. When her business is doing good and the struggles are less, that is not what fuels our heroine. Circumstances are always changing. Real Estate markets crash. Fortunes are won and lost in an instant. But, Joan is still joyful and smiles at the future.

Keep your life free from the love of money,

and be content with what you have,

for he has said,

"I will never leave you nor forsake you."

So we can confidently say,

"The Lord is my helper; I will not fear;
what can man do to me?"
Hebrews 13:5-6

Joan is not a lover of money. She is a lover of God and of people who are made in His image. That is how she is fearless. That is how her joy bubbles out as she lights up every room she enters. That is why strangers fall in love with her.

That is why children know they are safe in her arms. Joan walks in the Light. Her love for everyone around her, despite the pain, despite the critiques, evident for all to see.

Whoever says he is in the light
and hates his brother is still in darkness.
Whoever loves his brother
abides in the light,
and in him there is no cause for stumbling.

But whoever hates his brother

is in the darkness

and walks in the darkness,

and does not know where he is going,

because the darkness has blinded his eyes.

1 John 1:9-11

God's love is deep and wide. His love comforts her and carries her through the storms of life. And because of this great Love, Joan can take care of her household and joyfully live out her faith. This faith, her gift, that is lovely to see.

Chapter 11: The Blessed Woman

Her children rise up and call her blessed;
her husband also, and he praises her:

"Many women have done excellently,
but you surpass them all."

Proverbs 31:28-29

For seventeen long years Joan was a young, faithful widow. She worked with willing hands. She took care of her household and ran her business well. Her children certainly all rose up and called her blessed. We saw, better than anyone, the woman our mother was and is. She deserves our praise.

As we entered adulthood one by one we marveled at her excellence more and more. Through trials of our own we remembered how she weathered hers. This faithful woman who never let us down.

After seventeen years of hardship and pain, times of want and times of plenty, Joan found herself finally walking into her own love story when she least expected it.

She was her usual chipper self as she darted across the grocery store parking lot one sunny day. She threw her bags in her vehicle and, quick as a flash, pushed her shopping cart with all her might into the row of carts in her usual hurried way; she is forever always needing to get back to her office.

But, in her haste, she hadn't noticed the missing bar at the end of the line that was meant to stop the carts in their tracks. With her strong arms she had accidentally pushed the row of carts hard into a truck parked in front of them.

"Oops!" she shouted as the man in the truck slowly slid out. He couldn't be a bit angry at this youthful, smiling face. In her 50s her beauty was as radiant as ever. Inside and out. She made a quick, embarrassed apology to this stranger and returned to her office without knowing the impression she had made.

But, Terry was hooked. The next day he walked into her office hoping to learn more about this mysterious beauty. He had noticed the name of the business on her nametag when they met on that fateful day. He was fairly new to town and had no idea who this woman was. He didn't know she was the owner of the business, just that she worked there. He didn't know about her past or the myriad of rumors in constant circulation about her and her late husband. He only saw her. And he was drawn like a moth to a flame.

To her bright smile and dancing eyes. He had to know more.

After their first date they were both hooked. Terry was a widower from Florida who had raised five children of his own. They discovered they had a lot in common. They both possessed a quiet kind of faith and the hardest work ethic I've ever seen. Their romance was sweet.

And when the locals thought they needed to whisper all the floating rumors into his ear, he simply laughed. Terry had also lived through great pain and tragedy. Great trials that had refined his faith and judgment well. He had been around long enough to know how silly people can be. Though she was thought of as a Black Widow, by some very misinformed individuals because of her tragic past, Terry was smart enough to see the jewel he had found. Joan was real. With nothing to hide.

Our beautiful Joan was finally walking into her own love story once again…

Their eleven children between them were happy for the happy couple. Terry had walked a hard road as well. It was time for their happiness to begin. And so, Joan became his excellent wife. After seventeen years of widowhood. Joan was once again a wife.

During her years of widowhood, I had prayed for God to send Joan a worthy husband. This beautiful, shining, young widow who was an excellent wife. As her children grew and her house became empty, I would dream of mom finding someone to grow old with. She took such amazing care of us. And, as we all went on to live our own lives, I couldn't help but wonder what God might have up His sleeve for this beloved widow.

Amazingly, He did have something planned for her. Something most of us only read about in the storybooks. I never imagined He had a widower who had lived a life so similar to Joan's. Her perfect match.

Their wedding day was absolutely incredible. Completely different from her first wedding. Such a long way from that malnourished eighteen-year-old country girl from the dusty hills of north Georgia. That young naïve girl getting married to a stranger in a tiny country church, in the middle of nowhere, without one member of the groom's family in attendance.

This wedding was exactly opposite. Truly a sight to see. It was simple, yet elegant. The large church packed beyond seating capacity with smiling faces. Joan, the most stunning bride I've ever laid eyes on. Her glittering aura seemed to glide down that aisle as she stopped to hand each of her children a single red rose. Always thinking of us. Always loving us.

And so, after years of dancing alone in her joy, Joan finally had a partner to dance with.

Joan and Terry's dancing was absolutely magical. As they floated across the dancefloor together all eyes were glued to the shining couple. We couldn't help but hold our breath. Both sides of the family, and all in attendance, were mesmerized. We knew the hard road of suffering these two individuals had traveled to get to this one moment. The crowd who came to see our young widow all watched in silence, all wondering if this really was the happy ending for our God-loving heroine.

Can there really be happy endings?

Yes. There really are happy endings. God has given Joan her happy ending after all. And it is sweet. There is a time for everything under the sun. A time for every season. And Joan has lived through them all with a smile on her face. Joy in her heart. Faith firmly holding it all together in perfect harmony. Now is the time for Joan to dance…

For everything there is a season,

and a time for every matter under heaven:

A time to be born, and a time to die;

a time to plant,

and a time to pluck up what has been planted;

a time to kill, and a time to heal;

a time to break down, and a time to build up;

a time to weep, and a time to laugh;

a time to mourn, and a time to dance;

a time to cast away stones,

and a time to gather stones together,

a time to embrace,

and a time to refrain from embracing;

a time to seek, and a time to lose;

a time to keep, and a time to cast away;

a time to tear, and a time to sew;

a time to keep silence, and a time to speak;

a time to love, and a time to hate;

a time for war, and a time for peace.

Ecclesiastes 3:1-8

Joan's life has been marked with great suffering. But her suffering has produced even greater faith. Rock solid faith in the One Person who never let her down. During seasons of mourning or seasons of dancing, He has been faithful to her. He carried her when she needed to be carried, and now He dances with her in her joy.

Solomon, the wisest man to ever live, apart from Jesus, noticed this about life when he said, '[t]here is nothing better for a person than that he should eat and drink and find enjoyment in his toil. This also, I saw, is from the hand of God, for apart from Him who can eat or who can have enjoyment? For the one who pleases Him God has given wisdom and knowledge and joy…'

This is part of the great mystery of life that even Solomon could not quite grasp. He thought everything was a 'striving after the wind.'

But we know the rest of the story.

The rest of the story says that God became Man and has given us more to look forward to. Though we can enjoy this life and the fruits of our labor; we can also be joyful in the midst of pain because Christ has set us free. We are no longer afraid of what man can do to us. We are no longer afraid of never having a happy ending. We are looking heavenward, knowing our true home is there.

Joan dances here, with her new husband whom she loves, not only because of her happiness in the here and now, but because of her hope for eternity. Her faith shines bright still. Whether her circumstances are bright or bleak, her faith shines still.

***

And so, her children rise up and call her blessed. She raised us well. Loved us well. Taught us well. Modeling Jesus for us always. Pointing us to her Savior.

And now, her new husband also rises up and calls her blessed. He knows Joan's excellence. He sees her worth is far more precious than jewels. She is a sight to see. A woman full of compassion and love for everyone. A light walking among this dark world. She pierces the darkness every where she goes. Terry knows her worth.

His children also rise up and call her blessed. These souls that our mom has eagerly adopted into her full family. She makes time for all of us. Loving everyone with her overflowing abundance of God's love. They see her worth, too. And know she is a precious jewel.

And today, her multitude of grandchildren who multiply with each passing year, her inheritance from the Lord, also rise up and call her blessed.

Where Joan was surrounded for so many years with young children depending on her for their survival, she is now surrounded with adult children and grandchildren, multiplied ten-fold, all wanting to bless her. This woman who has surpassed all others in our eyes. Our mother. Our nana. Our friend. The gorgeous, unassuming young widow who is the heroine of all our stories.

Chapter 12:

The Poor Widow

Charm is deceitful, and beauty is vain,
but a woman who fears the LORD is to be praised.

Give her of the fruit of her hands,
and let her works praise her in the gates.
Proverbs 31:30-31

And Jesus sat over against the treasury,
and beheld how the people cast money into the treasury:
and many that were rich cast in much.

And there came a certain poor widow,
and she threw in two mites,
which make a farthing.

And he called unto him his disciples,
and saith unto them,

Verily I say unto you,
That this poor widow hath cast more in,
than all they which have cast into the treasury:

For they did cast in of their abundance;
but she of her want did cast in all that she had,
even all her living.

Mark 12:41-44 (KJV)

In all the years I read the story of the *Widow's Mite* in the bible, I had always pictured an incredibly old woman walking into that temple, hunched over, possibly at the end of her days. One day this woman miraculously changed right before my eyes.

When Jesus pointed her out, and called His disciples to pay attention to her, I finally looked and saw who she was. She was my own mother. Not old at all. But very young and beautiful. At the beginning of her days, not the end. Standing tall with her shoulders erect. Her face was radiant and shining bright. Lighting up the room as she quietly slipped in to give her offering to the King of the universe.

As I watched in silence, sitting with Jesus and His disciples, my heart began to race. I watched my mother's graceful arm reach out and drop in those two tiny mites, barely worth a penny. Her eyes were dancing and a smile was on her face. There was no sadness as I had always wrongfully perceived. For she was a joyful giver. Thankful for what she had. And more thankful to give than receive.

When she walked by, her gaze lingered on the King sitting among us. Jesus. Having eyes for Him only. Their eyes locked and He smiled at her. And her smile grew wider still as she kept her eyes on Him. Her look was not a proud look, but a look of dignity and strength. A look of love and loyalty. Jesus simply nodded as she passed by. There was an electric current between them the rest of us could only guess about. She knew this God-Man and He knew her. She was not unnoticed by her King and Lord. They were old friends. And it showed in their exchange.

She didn't need to be congratulated in that moment by Him. She could see He was busy trying to teach the rest of us something. And she had work to do anyway. Mouths to feed. Bills to pay. Gardens to tend. Love to share. When Her master returned she knew to be ready. He would find her managing His accounts well. All would be in order. Nothing out of place. Living up to what He called her to do. Looking forward to His coming…

"But concerning that day and hour
no one knows,
not even the angels of heaven,
nor the Son, but the Father only.

For as were the days of Noah,
so will be the coming of the Son of Man.
For as in those days before the flood
they were eating and drinking,
marrying and giving in marriage,
until the day Noah entered the ark,
and they were unaware until the flood came
and swept them all away,
so will be the coming of the Son of Man.

Then two men will be in the field;
one will be taken and one left.
Two women will be grinding at the mill;
one will be taken and one left.
Therefore, stay awake,
for you do not know on what day
your Lord is coming.

But know this,

that if the master of the house had known

in what part of the night the thief was coming,

he would have stayed awake

and would not let his house be broken into.

Therefore you also must be ready,

for the Son of Man is coming

at an hour you do not expect.

Who then is the faithful and wise servant,

whom his master has set over his household,

to give them food at their proper time?

Blessed is that servant

whom his master will find

so doing when he comes.

Truly, I say to you,

he will set him over all his possessions.

But if that wicked servant says to himself,

'My master is delayed,'

and begins to beat his fellow servants
and eats and drinks with drunkards,

the master of that servant
will come on a day
when he does not expect him
and at an hour he does not know

and will cut him in pieces
and put him with the hypocrites.

In that place there will be weeping
and gnashing of teeth."
Matthew 24:36-50

This is a difficult text to read. We want to only think of God's goodness. Not His eternal judgement.

But, in our wondering at His complexities we can still have faith in our Creator. For the moral of this story is that God's ways are higher than our ways. His complexities far more than we could ever fathom.

The Creator of heaven and earth came down in the form of a Man. Jesus. Who came and loved us and taught us how to live. He lived the perfect life we just can't seem to ever live up to, and then willingly sacrificed Himself by taking God's wrath for us. For God is a just God. And there must be justice for our wrong doing. But please don't miss the Good News. *The gospel of grace.* Notice Jesus willingly stood in our place and received our just punishment. Grace simply means: undeserved merit. Us 'undeserving' people have hope because of Him… We did nothing. *He did it all.*

Jesus died and was buried. In our place. But He didn't stay in that grave.

The rumors are still passed around to this day that His disciples came and stole His body in the middle of the night. The weary fisherman, who didn't even know how to use a sword, overtook a legion of trained Roman soldiers, who more than likely looked like they could have played in the movie *300*.

It's funny how rumors fly when people just don't want to believe the truth.

The truth here is Jesus. He is who He says He is. God, wrapped in flesh. Jesus. The maker of heaven and earth. The beginning and the end. Alive and well after completely defeating death. The God-Man walked out of that grave by His own power. And today Jesus, the Son, is seated at the right hand of the Father, judging the hearts of man.

When we read hard scripture, our default is to push back and try to fully understand the mind of God. When life is too hard, we want to scream at the One we know deep down is in control of it all.

I love the book of Job for this very reason. Job was a man who lived through many, many trials. He was stripped bare of all he had held dear and told to curse God by those around him. Yet, he did not. He did, however, question God's goodness. God's answer will surprise you. When God spoke out of the whirlwind, poor Job could only cup his hands over his prideful mouth and stand in awe of His Creator.

He realized when God spoke just how little he actually understood. How little he knew. Job realized he was not there when God was making everything out of nothing. He was not standing at the beginning of time by the Father's side creating. Neither was I. Scripture says Jesus was there.

The gospel of John actually starts out by telling us this great truth.

'In the beginning was the Word,
and the Word was with God,
and the Word was God.

He was in the beginning with God.

All things were made through Him,

and without Him

was not any thing made that was made…

…And the Word became flesh

and dwelt among us,

and we have seen His glory,

glory as of the only Son from the Father,

full of grace and truth.'

John 1:1-3, 14

Jesus is always our answer to the really tough questions. To the questions that hurt us and make us want to scream from the very real pain.

Joan, my mother, the poor widow who still loved her King, has taught me through her actions to never question God in a way that leads to disbelief. God is good. Despite the pain. God is just. Despite the injustices. God is faithful. Despite others' hypocrisy. He is worthy of our faith and unwavering devotion. Even when we don't understand it all. He is worthy still.

This widow I love, whom Jesus pointed out and praised, is the best kind of teacher. She is the best kind of teacher because she doesn't teach what she does not know. No one can say she doesn't understand pain. No one can say she hasn't walked through the fire. No one can say she is happy only because she has lived an easy life.

On the contrary, she has known the deepest of sorrows and terrifyingly terrible pain. She has walked through the refining fire and come out the other side shining bright. She is happy and free.

Free because Jesus has set her free. And happy simply because she chooses to be happy. Joan believes happiness is a choice to be made each waking day. And it will always be her choice. She does not choose to wallow in her pain or circumstances. She chooses to be joyful and to dance happily in the rain that her Lord sends on the just and the unjust.

Our beautiful, young, poor widow. Willing to give all she had to Jesus. When there was nothing to give, she gave still. When there was no hope, she knew Hope was a Person. When her world was dark, she followed the Light. Joan. The God-loving heroine rightfully deserving our praise. Our young widow, leading the way with all her might. Truly, a wonder to behold.

Those of us who know her count ourselves blessed. We lived with her through the hardest times and watched her go. We learned from her and were loved by her. Really, we are the lucky ones. I wish I could say we were easy on her. But, the truth is, we were the worst kind of kids and only made things harder for Joan.

And so, in the aftermath, we can simply turn to this incredible woman who happens to be our mother, our glowing, young, poor widow who gave all she had, and sheepishly say, "Thanks mom."

You forever will be our hero.

The End

Soli Deo Gloria!

Epilogue

Today you will still find Joan working away in her real estate office. Still as beautiful as ever boasting her radiant smile. Busy being the older woman described in scripture, modeling for us younger women how to live a life worthy to be praised.

Her orphaned children are all grown and living lives they can only hope represent their amazing, heroic mother well. Joan's eldest daughter went to work with her as soon as she could and has been an instrumental part in building the company into what it is today.

Joan's second daughter, always the fashionista, now owns a successful women's clothing boutique in the downtown area of their hometown, rightfully called, *Rumors.*

Joan and Tom's only son has grown into a man who looks like his dad; exhibiting his adventurous spirit coupled with Joan's faithful personality. He has had a successful career in the United States Air Force and makes us all ridiculously proud.

Joan's baby daughter went on to follow in her parent's footsteps of being the family environmentalist. She is currently a leading land conservationist in western North Carolina working hard to save the land our parents loved so much.

Our baby brother, our gift in a time of great darkness, has continued to pull at our heartstrings through the years. If only he could know just how much we all love him. Words can never express. He is about to be a college graduate and step into the big bad world. But, I know he will be fine. He will be more than fine. As we all are, because of our mother, Joan. Our

God-loving heroine who has always been there for us. Shining the Light onto our dark paths. Showing us the way through her actions. Loving us no matter what.

And as for me? Tom and Joan's third daughter? Well, I'm the writer of this story. Just a small author who is simply trying to emulate THE AUTHOR and perfecter of our faith. To God be the glory. Amen.

Pictured above: The author with her mother, Joan.

Pictured below: Joan with her six children standing in birth order at her surprise 60th birthday party bash in their hometown.

Joan surrounded by her seven adult children,

including her baby sister whom she also raised.

About the author

CJP Navarro lives near Asheville, NC. Married to her college sweetheart, Jesse, and full-time mom to Joey, Jeremiah, Brick, Baylon and Crosby. With a degree in photojournalism and a true love for the Word of God, her passion has always been sharing real life stories and how they apply to scripture. When she is not writing, the bulk of her days consist of being a soccer mom and chasing her hilarious twin toddlers around the house while expertly dodging large piles of laundry. The laundry never ends…

My mother has always encouraged me to write. It is an absolute honor to pay some sort of small tribute to her life in this way. She told me it was time to start writing when I turned thirty. And, in my usual rebellious way, I started when I was thirty-five. Thanks mom, for always being my biggest fan.

Love, c.

References:

Other titles by author CJP Navarro:

Encompass (sold on Amazon.com)

Thorns and Thistles (coming soon)

You may contact the author at:

cjpnavarro@gmail.com

Or mail inquiries to:

Faithless Daughter Ministries

P.O. Box 644

Columbus, NC 28722

Thorns & Thistles

Written by: CJP Navarro

Chapter 1: Cursed

My eight-year-old son looks at me with his wide, clear blue eyes and I smile. I love this child more than I can express. I love to look at pictures of him because the only time he is sitting still is when he is forever frozen, framed in time hanging neatly on my wall. In reality, he is my hardest child. Not because he is a problem child, but because the depths of his mind and soul seem to far exceed my own. His energy is absolutely limitless next to my own dwindling physical abilities. Even in my prime I did not come close to possessing his stamina. He never stops moving. Never stops thinking. Never stops talking…

Driving home now from a doctor appointment he chatters away, firing off his probing questions at me as we have this rare moment alone.

We drive up our winding road, the scenery as perfect as ever, while he rattles off question after question about the deep things in life. I am trying to pay attention, but it is so hard. My mind likes to wander, too. He talks to me like I would talk to a friend. Rattling off life's big questions and philosophically deciphering God's greatest mysteries.

And so, I try in this moment to be a friend to my son and listen to his chatter that is really important to him.

The day is beautiful as the setting sun peaks through the now green trees. The leaves have only just started coming back to life. They are bright green and small enough to allow light through. It's magical as we pass the rushing waterfall cascading down the side of our mountain. I breathe it in deeply and try to just enjoy this moment with my deep-thinking chatter-box beside me. No matter how many times I pass this water as it falls dangerously close to our road, I still have to slow down to nearly a stop and take it all in. Moving water. Living water. The enticing fresh smell of it all reminding me of the goodness of God.

But, my sweet child perched beside me has no idea of my thoughts and keeps chattering away, drowning out the effect of cascading perfection that I'm trying to attain. And, if I'm completely honest with my sinful self, I just want silence from him so I can be lost in my own thoughts. He is interrupting my own dreaming heart. Just when I think he will stop, he revs up again. Like that old bunny commercial from when I was a kid…he just keeps going and going and going…

I give up as I let off the brake pedal and accelerate forward. Toward home and back to the reality that is my life as I try to listen to this little energizer bunny who will apparently never stop. I really do try to pay attention. I try to be sincere. But, I sincerely, sinfully, selfishly feel him as nothing more than a giant thorn in my side. Always poking me. As if the very finger of God is annoyingly, relentlessly poking at my selfishness in these all too frequent moments of weakness.

As I silently wish for the noise in my ear to stop, I am suddenly startled by the question my son asks, that I only half hear, and my thoughts swirl back to this little boy beside me. Does he read my mind? No. But God does. My son wants to know why there are thorns in this world. They have no real purpose he says. No purpose *what-so-ever.* And they hurt. Really, really bad. My mind springs into action as this question brings me hurling out of my own daydreams and sinful intentions.

Thorns?

Yes. Thorns. Why do we have thorns? What a great question!

The answer floods my mind as if the bible is speaking audibly in that moment of realization. I flip ferociously in my memory back to the very beginning as I grip the steering wheel tighter and search for an answer to this deep and very valid question. The pages flittering fast in my mind and heart. The words that have been written on them long ago flooding my head as I drive and think as quickly as possible.

My son has stopped talking now. Patiently waiting for me to answer. He expects an answer. Though he wants to hear what I will say, I suspect deep down he already knows it. My deep thinker. This child of mine who says he will be a missionary or a preacher one day. There is such a rich sincerity in his tone and raw compassion in his actions toward others that I actually believe him. And, though his emotions run deep and are hard for him to control at this stage in his life, he does seem to be called to God's deep thinking and passionately seeks answers to life's struggles. He has always been my hardest child to rear, yet, I can clearly see the gifts God has endowed to this little man; if he would only choose to use them one day.

As we drive on my thoughts take me back a few thousand years ago to the garden where life as we know it all started. Genesis. The very first book in God's Word. These ancient words penned by Moses that are written on my heart and mind jump at me. Beckoning me to notice something this sweet little chatter-box is trying to illustrate for those of us who are slower to see.

He takes me past God's beautiful, perfect creation. That amazing paradise we lost. The utopia that we are forever searching for. That mystical place we just can't seem to ever regain. Here, in that lost paradise, are where my thoughts land. And here, we step into the saddest day ever recorded in earth's history.

Ken Ham, founder and president of Answers in Genesis, was the first person I ever heard describe the fall like that. And, he is right. The day our first parents chose to sin was the saddest day in history because we lost something. Everything actually. The paradise we've been looking for ever since was lost in that one moment.

That one choice that brought

the curse

upon our heads…

And to Adam [God] said,

"Because you have listened to the voice of your wife
and have eaten of the tree which I commanded you,

'You shall not eat of it,'

cursed is the ground because of you;
in pain you shall eat of it all the days of your life;

thorns and thistles it shall bring forth for you;
and you shall eat the plants of the field.

By the sweat of your face you shall eat bread,
till you return to the ground,

for out of it you were taken;

for you are dust,
and to dust you shall return."

Genesis 3:17-19

Cursed. The ground is cursed I tell my inquisitive eight-year-old. Sin entered God's perfect creation and because of our sin the ground became cursed. Thorns and thistles sprang up and started hurting us.

My child has taught me something today. The thorns that seemingly have no purpose, have immense purpose after all.

***

All of my children, not just my inquisitive eight-year-old, seem to be born into being my little consciences walking around, seeing every move I make. They see all of my sin, and I cringe as they innocently point it out, knowing how right they are. I can't seem to hide from them. They know me so well.

And so, I slowly begin to learn how to welcome their prodding. The long days that turn slowly into years and years of these little eyes watching every move I make. Causing me to constantly consider my actions compared to my words. It seems God Himself is encouraging this dance.

In being alone, which is the state I truly prefer, it is so easy to hide the imperfections from myself.

So, what if I eat a whole bag of salty, yummy potato chips while I sit on the couch binge watching my favorite show? In my mind I easily convince myself that it's perfectly fine, as long as nobody sees. The lights are turned low and the dark seems to entice the hidden sinfulness to come out and play. Oops. Did I eat the whole bag? Oh well. It's easy to shrug off in that dark place.

So, what if I hit the snooze button fifteen times before finally jumping out of bed and then running late the rest of the day? No one knows why I'm running behind except me. If I smile big enough everything is fine. I'm just late for normal reasons like slow traffic, or a wreck right in front of me. But, the real truth of the matter is: *I'm the wreck.*

Having children in my life makes me come face to face with the reality that is my wreck of a self. I can't just tell them about right and wrong; they see it in me. I am their model. Whether I like it or not. Their curious minds want to know what I am eating and why. If I can have it then why can't they, their inquisitive minds want to know. But, when I see them eating a whole bag of chips, or skittles, or chocolate, or whatever, I gasp and exclaim that they can't possibly do that. I start to see my own imperfections in them and it cuts me to my core. God uses them, my sweet blessings from above, to get to me.

When I lie in bed hitting the snooze button, wanting to just close my eyes and return to my dreams, there is a little finger poking me. It might as well be the finger of God Himself. But, in this reality it is simply my sweet two-year-old. Wanting a 'snack' at 6am. I sigh as the scripture I know so well floods my mind. I was a dutiful mom after all and diligently taught God's Word to my blessings. But, teaching it to them has allowed it to also fill my own heart and soul. Which isn't always convenient when I want to return to my sinful, fleshy self…

Go to the ant, O sluggard;
consider her ways,
and be wise.

Without having any chief, officer, or ruler,
she prepares her bread in summer
and gathers her food for harvest.

How long will you lie there, O sluggard?
When will you arise from your sleep?

A little sleep, a little slumber,
a little folding of the hands to rest,

and poverty will come upon you like a robber,
and want like an armed man.

Proverbs 6:6-11

Okay. Yes. I have taught this to my children in a planned out and perfectly tidy little bible study around our kitchen table. But do I live it out on a daily basis in front of them? I just want to sleep and not face my day. But, that little finger keeps poking. God keeps waking me up. His Words ringing so true in my ears. When I want to ignore the gift of today, my little world turns upside down. Poverty comes upon me like a robber and want like an armed man who swiftly steals my peace and joy.

One of my toddlers takes matters into his own hands and finds the giant bag of chips I have just purchased at the store. They are veggie chips. A 'healthier' version of my sinful little habit. The bag is almost as big as he is. He skillfully totes it from the cupboard all the way to my bedside and as I lazily turn over in my comfy, sluggard loving sheets I see the disaster as it unfolds right before my groggy eyes. This gift of a day regrettably begins with seeing him carrying the open bag upside down.

Somehow, he has managed to not spill one chip until he reaches me where it finally all comes crashing to the floor in its lovely, salty glory. The saltiness I crave is now covering the once clean floor of my beloved bedroom. I try to lunge for the bag, but it is to no avail as my giant pregnant belly prevents me from doing so. He quickly jumps back as he says the cutest 'uh oh' I've ever heard and we just stare at one another in disbelief. The Mother of all Sluggards and her little, sweet, beautiful, incredibly hungry conscience of a toddler both wishing this day had started out very different.

When I choose to be lazy, my days are turned upside down. Everything spills out of everywhere and the mess is the chaos of my life. I just wanted a 'little' more sleep. But, the peacefulness of my home has been stolen suddenly by the robber who steals when we least expect it. Caught completely, helplessly, hopelessly unaware by that old thief who loves to steal our joy.

Out of bed finally, I remorsefully walk into a chaotic day. A chaotic day that, when I'm completely honest, was caused by me. This wreck of a wife and mother who desperately needs a Savior. All I can think is how much easier it is for me to be alone. I remember the days I use to live alone longingly as I can see that spotless apartment I called home. Where nothing was moved out of place when I wasn't looking. Where everything was bright and clean. Where I could sleep as long as I wanted. The selfishness of it all creeping into my heart causing a dark shadow to rise. Casting a cloud over God's brilliant Light.

It is so much easier for me to be alone.

But, thankfully God knew it isn't good for us to be left alone. He wants us living in community for good reason. He wants my little children poking me with their little fingers. My blessings from the Lord. My little thorns that prick my heart. My little thorns that poke at me when I just want to hide under the covers. My precious, beautiful little thorns. Diligently pointing out my desperate need for rescue. My desperate need for the Savior.

***

The rain continues to fall. Our tiny county has been in a state of emergency for the past week from flash flooding and outrageous mudslides barreling down the hillsides. Roads are destroyed. Homes are smashed and vacated.

Still, it rains.

Moments like this remind me of our incredible God. Moments like this also take me all the way back to the beginning. Back to Genesis. It reminds me of the first flood and His promise to never destroy the whole earth again in that way.

People often tell me there wasn't a global flood. And I hear them. But, my answer is always the same. I just want them to ponder the possibility. On days like today, when a little water devastates a local area. When mountains are literally moved, large interstates buckle and people's lives are washed away; can they just for a second allow their mind to rest on the immensity of what a GLOBAL flood would have looked like?

Local floods devastate. A global flood would have absolutely annihilated.

These are the thorns and thistles causing us to remember the curse. Though God has kept His promise of never sending a global flood again, there are localized floods all over this shrinking planet we call home. Local floods reminding us of the sin once washed away. Thorns and thistles pricking us, hurting us, causing us to look up or to wallow in the mud.

I am not saying God is mean. We can never lose sight of His goodness, though it can be overshadowed by our sin and brokenness. Living in a cursed world hurts immensely. Adam and Eve went their own way and essentially wanted to be their own god. Like a distraught toddler, they basically just wanted what *they* wanted.

And so, our wise Parent gave us what we wanted. Unfortunately, like a stubborn child who just touched a hot oven their loving parent tried to warn them about, we tend to discover all too late sometimes that our own way is the way leading to pain. Left to our own devices we will wallow in the mud that we can't dig our way out of and simply wonder at the difficulties. Left to our own devices we might sleep the gift of today away or sit in the dark eating an entire bag of chips, only to wake in the morning light with a massive belly ache.

As the rain inevitably falls in this life, on my tiny place in the world, I look up into the heavens and remember His glory. I let the rain wash me and cleanse me as it was meant to do. I take my eyes off the mud as it rolls down my feet and look up to the heavens. My arms instinctively lift in worship. Knowing the blue sky lies beyond the thick gray of this moment. I look heavenward. Allowing the thorns and thistles in my life to point me to Him. These thorns that we all have.

Even the Apostle Paul records that he prayed fervently for God to remove 'the thorn from his side.' Yet, he goes on to share with us how God never did.

Why?

Because the thorns in our lives always keep us on our knees. Looking heavenward. Looking to our Heavenly Father for true comfort. Lasting comfort.

An ill-tempered child or a difficult parent. A next-door neighbor continuously causing you daily stress. A husband who seems aloof and out of touch. A wife who shows no respect. A work colleague or boss that causes you dread each waking day. The things that keep you up at night. These are thorns in our side. Put there to turn our hearts to Him.

I am slowly learning that we must face the curse, instead of hiding from it or pretending it isn't there, if we are to find true relief. Cursed is the ground because of poor Adam. The first man who made a really bad choice. Our world is cursed and broken whether we try to hide under the covers or not. Full of thorns and thistles that really do hurt. Hurting us for a purpose we need to know.

And so, this story begins by going back to the real beginning and trying to make sense of it all. Hoping to be enlightened and discover something I feel my deep-thinking eight-year-old son already knows…

Thorns & Thistles by author CJP Navarro

Coming soon…

www.ingramcontent.com/pod-product-compliance
Lightning Source LLC
Chambersburg PA
CBHW021925040426
42448CB00008B/920
9781732280618